CW00523402

AFTER DERRIDA

AFTER DERRIDA

Nicholas Royle

Manchester University Press

Manchester and New York

distributed exclusively in the USA
and Canada by St Martin's Press

Copyright © Nicholas Royle 1995

Published by Manchester University Press
Oxford Road, Manchester M13 9NR, UK
and Room 400, 175 Fifth Avenue, New York, NY 10010, USA

Distributed exclusively in the USA and Canada by St. Martin's Press, Inc.,
175 Fifth Avenue, New York, NY 10010, USA

British Library Cataloguing-in-Publication Data
A catalogue record is available from the British Library

Library of Congress Cataloging-in-Publication Data
Royle, Nicholas, 1957– .
After Derrida/Nicholas Royle.
p.   cm.
Includes bibliographical references and index.
ISBN 0–7190–4378–6. — ISBN 0–7190–4379–4 (pbk).
1. Criticism. 2. Derrida, Jacques — Contributions in criticism.
3. Psychoanalysis and literature. 4. Deconstruction.
5. Literature — History and criticism — Theory, etc. I. Title.
PN81.R69 1995
801'.95—dc20

94–5404
CIP

ISBN 0 7190 4378 6 *hardback*

ISBN 0 7190 4379 4 *paperback*

Phototypeset by Intype, London
Printed in Great Britain
by Biddles Limited, Guildford and King's Lynn

For Kati

In Memory
of
Bill Readings
(1960–94)

Contents

Acknowledgements

In the essays that follow it may seem that nothing is said as regards that strange and neglected genre known as 'Acknowledgements'. More markedly perhaps even than a Preface, the Acknowledgements come at the beginning but are written at the end. Placing them at the end of the book, just before or right after the Index, would do little effectively in the way of acknowledging the paradoxes of 'acknowledgements'. In fact such a tactic would only be counter-productive with respect to *After Derrida* which is, at least for me, pervaded by the demands and impossibilities of acknowledgement, starting from the title. If it is impossible to provide adequate or appropriate acknowledgement of those whose love and friendship, conversation, criticism, thought and writing have made one's own work possible, it is also the case, at least for me, that the present study is in a sense nothing but acknowledgements. Acknowledgements engulf both writing and the book.

Such engulfment must begin with Bill Readings, whose tragically early death occurred between the time of my submitting the manuscript of this book and receiving the proofs. His writing and his friendship affected everything that I have tried to do in these pages. Without wishing to impose on them the slightest culpability for what may be imprecisely thought or unjustly said in this work, I would also like to express my particular thanks to Valerie Allen, Ares Axiotis, Andrew Bennett, Geoff Bennington, Rachel Bowlby, Tim Clark, Gerald Doherty, Maud Ellmann, Markku Eskelinen, Michael Gasson, Jacqueline Hall, Sally Hornicoe, Julian Hosie, Asko Kauppinen, Peter Krapp, Richard Lansdown, Dan McAdam, Robert Penhallurick, David Punter, Caroline Rooney, Anita Roy, Kathleen Royle, Maxwell Royle, Alan Shima, Ann Wordsworth and Robert Young. For further stimulation and support in relation to specific chapters or aspects of this book, I am very grateful to Derek Attridge, Leo Bersani, Mikkel Borch-Jacobsen, Scott Brewster, Lucille Cairns, John Drakakis, Paul Green, Geoffrey Hartman, Frank Kermode, Peter Larkin, Albert Leventure, John Llewelyn, J. Hillis Miller, Samantha Penwarden, Tina Webberley, Sarah Wood and Elizabeth Wright. This book would be unimaginable without the institutional and pedagogical contexts out of which (in perhaps a double sense) it has been written: I should like to record my gratitude to all my colleagues and students, both at the University of Tampere, in Finland, and more recently at the University of Stirling, in Scotland. Finally I would like simply to remark in passing that Robert Smith's *Derrida and Autobiography* (Cambridge University Press, 1995) forms an indispensable supplement to the present volume.

Various parts of this book, at various stages of its quasi-complete-ness, have been presented as papers at seminars or conferences. I am especially grateful to those willing to listen — and in some cases make (what were for me) invaluable comments — at the Department of English, University of Uppsala; King's College, Cambridge; the University of Oulu, Finland; the Instituto Superior de Psicologia Aplicada, Lisbon; the Centre for Research in Philosophy and Literature, University of Warwick; the Department of English Studies, University of Tampere; the Foreign Body seminar, University of Stirling; the Department of English, Saint David's University College at Lampeter, University of Wales; the Department of English, University College of Swansea, University of Wales; the Depart-ment of English Studies, University of Southampton; All Souls, Oxford; and the Critical Theory seminar at the University College of Cardiff, University of Wales. In the case of Chapter 7, 'Foreign Body: "The decon-struction of a pedagogical institution and all that it implies" ', I have made little attempt to alter it from the final form in which it was given as a paper, at the Cardiff Critical Theory seminar in March 1994. Other chapters, too, may retain traces of the originally 'oral' nature of their dispersal. I hope that this may be felt to comport with the emphasis which this study puts on the performative as well as the descriptive, or rather on an unsettling of distinctions between the two.

An earlier version of Chapter 5 was published as 'The Distraction of "Freud": Literature, Psychoanalysis and the Bacon–Shakespeare Controversy', in the *Oxford Literary Review*, vol. 12 (1990). Part of Chapter 6 appeared, in a rather different form, under the title 'The Love of Reading: "A Postcard from the Volcano" ', in *Literature and Psychology*, the Proceedings of the Ninth International Conference on Literature and Psychoanalysis, ed. Frederico Pereira (Lisbon: Instituto Superior de Psic-ologia Aplicada, 1993). An earlier version of Chapter 8, 'On Not Reading: Derrida and Beckett', was published in *Reading Reading: Essays on the Theory and Practice of Reading*, ed. Andrew Bennett (Tampere: Tampere English Studies, 1993). I am grateful to the editors and publishers for permission to reprint.

Acknowledgement should also be made here to Margaret Connolly Associates, Carcanet Press and Farrar, Strauss and Giroux Inc, for per-mission to cite Les Murray's 'Mollusc'; and to Faber and Faber Ltd and Alfred A. Knopf Inc, for permission to cite Wallace Stevens's 'A Postcard from the Volcano'.

Abbreviations of works cited

Abbreviations of works by Jacques Derrida

AC 'Aphorism Countertime', trans. Nicholas Royle, in *Acts of Literature*, ed. Derek Attridge (London and New York: Routledge, 1992), 414–33

Aft 'Afterw.rds: or, at least, less than a letter about a letter less', trans. Geoffrey Bennington, in *Afterwords*, ed. Nicholas Royle (Tampere, Finland: Outside Books, 1992), 197–203

AT 'Of an Apocalyptic Tone Recently Adopted in Philosophy', trans. John P. Leavey, Jr, *Oxford Literary Review*, 6:2 (1984), 3–37

ATED 'Afterword: Toward an Ethic of Discussion', trans. Samuel Weber, in *Limited Inc* (Evanston, Illinois: Northwestern University Press, 1988), 111–60

Bio 'Biodegradables', trans. Peggy Kamuf, *Critical Inquiry*, 15:4 (1989), 812–73

BL 'Border Lines', trans. James Hulbert, in Harold Bloom et al., *Deconstruction and Criticism* (New York: Seabury Press, 1979), 75–176

C *Cinders*, trans. Ned Lukacher (Lincoln: Nebraska University Press, 1991)

Che 'Che cos'è la poesia?', trans. Peggy Kamuf, in *A Derrida Reader: Between the Blinds*, ed. Kamuf (London and New York: Harvester, 1991), 221–37

D *Dissemination*, trans. Barbara Johnson (Chicago: Chicago University Press, 1981)

DA 'Deconstruction in America: An Interview with Jacques Derrida', trans. James Creech, *Critical Exchange*, 17 (1985), 1–33

DI 'Declarations of Independence', trans. Tom Keenan and Tom Pepper, *New Political Science*, 15 (1986), 7–15

Diff 'Différance', in *Margins of Philosophy*, trans. Alan Bass (Chicago: Chicago University Press, 1982), 1–27

DO 'Deconstruction and the Other', interview with Richard Kearney, in Kearney, *Dialogues with Contemporary Continental Thinkers* (Manchester: Manchester University Press, 1984), 105–26

DTB 'Des Tours de Babel', trans. Joseph F. Graham, in *Difference in Translation*, ed. Joseph F. Graham (Ithaca: Cornell University Press, 1985), 165–205

DTJ 'Deconstruction: A Trialogue in Jerusalem', *Mishkenot Sha'ananim Newsletter*, no.7 (December 1986), 1–7

E 'Envois', in *The Post Card: From Socrates to Freud and Beyond*, trans. Alan Bass (Chicago: Chicago University Press, 1987), 3–256

EM 'The Ends of Man', in *Margins of Philosophy*, trans. Alan Bass (Chicago: Chicago University Press, 1982), 109–36

EO *The Ear of the Other: Otobiography, Transference, Translation*, trans. Peggy Kamuf, ed. Christie V. McDonald (New York: Schocken Books, 1985)

F '*Fors*: The Anglish Words of Nicolas Abraham and Maria Torok', trans. Barbara Johnson, in Abraham and Torok, *The Wolf Man's Magic Word: A Cryptonymy*, trans. Nicholas Rand (Minneapolis: University of Minnesota Press, 1986), xi-xlviii

FL 'Force of Law: The "Mystical Foundation of Authority" ', trans. Mary Quaintance, *Cardozo Law Review*, 11:5/6 (1990), 921–1045

FS 'Force and Signification', in *Writing and Difference*, trans. Alan Bass (London: Routledge and Kegan Paul, 1978), 3–30

FTA 'Fifty-Two Aphorisms for a Foreword', in *Deconstruction Omnibus Volume*, eds Andreas Papadakis, Catherine Cooke and Andrew Benjamin (London: Academy Editions, 1989), 67–9

G *Glas*, trans. John P. Leavey, Jr, and Richard Rand (Lincoln: Nebraska University Press, 1986)

IDCN 'In Discussion with Christopher Norris', in *Deconstruction Omnibus Volume*, eds Andreas Papadakis, Catherine Cooke and Andrew Benjamin (London: Academy Editions, 1989), 71–9

IJD 'An "Interview" with Jacques Derrida', *The Cambridge Review*, 113: 2318 (October 1992), 31–9

JD ii Jacques Derrida, 'Circumfession', in *Jacques Derrida*, trans. Geoffrey Bennington (Chicago: Chicago University Press, 1993)

LG 'The Law of Genre', trans. Avital Ronell, in *Acts of Literature*, ed. Derek Attridge (London and New York: Routledge, 1992), 221–52

LI 'Limited Inc a, b, c . . .', trans. Samuel Weber and Jeffrey Mehlman, in *Limited Inc* (Evanston, Illinois: Northwestern University Press, 1988), 29–110

LJF 'Letter to a Japanese Friend', trans. David Wood and Andrew Benjamin, in *A Derrida Reader: Between the Blinds*, ed. Peggy Kamuf (London and New York: Harvester, 1991), 270–6

LO   'Living On', trans. James Hulbert, in Harold Bloom et al., *Deconstruction and Criticism* (New York: Seabury Press, 1979), 75–176

LUNFP   'Let Us Not Forget — Psychoanalysis', trans. Geoffrey Bennington and Rachel Bowlby, *Oxford Literary Review*, 12 (1990), 3–7

M   Mémoires: for Paul de Man, trans. Cecile Lindsay, Jonathan Culler and Eduardo Cadava (New York: Columbia University Press, 1986)

MB   Memoirs of the Blind: The Self-Portrait and Other Ruins, trans. Pascale-Anne Brault and Michael Naas (Chicago: Chicago University Press, 1993)

Mo   'Mochlos; or, The Conflict of the Faculties', trans. Richard Rand and Amy Wygant, in *Logomachia: The Conflict of the Faculties*, ed. Richard Rand (Lincoln: Nebraska University Press, 1992), 3–34

NA   'No Apocalypse, Not Now (full speed ahead, seven missiles, seven missives)', trans. Catherine Porter and Philip Lewis, *Diacritics*, 14:2 (1984), 20–31

OCP   'On Colleges and Philosophy: Jacques Derrida with Geoff Bennington', in *Postmodernism: ICA Documents*, ed. Lisa Appignanesi (London: Free Association Books, 1989), 209–28

OG   Of Grammatology, trans. Gayatri Chakravorty Spivak (Baltimore: Johns Hopkins University Press, 1976)

OH   The Other Heading: Reflections on Today's Europe, trans. Pascale-Anne Brault and Michael B. Naas (Bloomington: Indiana University Press, 1992)

OS   Of Spirit: Heidegger and the Question, trans. Geoffrey Bennington and Rachel Bowlby (Chicago: Chicago University Press, 1989)

P   Positions, trans. Alan Bass (Chicago: Chicago University Press, 1981)

PC   The Post Card: From Socrates to Freud and Beyond, trans. Alan Bass (Chicago: Chicago University Press, 1987)

PIO   'Psyche: Inventions of the Other', trans. Catherine Porter, in *Reading de Man Reading*, eds Lindsay Waters and Wlad Godzich (Minneapolis: University of Minnesota Press, 1989)

POO   'Passions: "An Oblique Offering" ', trans. David Wood, in *Derrida: A Critical Reader*, ed. David Wood (Oxford and Cambridge, Mass.: Basil Blackwell, 1992), 5–35

PR   'The Principle of Reason: The University in the Eyes of Its Pupils', trans. Catherine Porter and Edward P. Morris, *Diacritics* 13:3 (1983), 3–20

Pro   'Proverb: "He that would pun . . . " ', Foreword to *Glassary* (Lincoln: Nebraska University Press, 1986), 17–20

PSAWV   'Post-Scriptum: Aporias, Ways and Voices', trans. John P. Leavey, Jr, in *Derrida and Negative Theology*, eds. Harold Coward and

Toby Foshay (Albany, New York: State University of New York Press, 1992), 283–323

QQ 'Qual Quelle: Valéry's Sources', in *Margins of Philosophy*, trans. Alan Bass (Chicago: Chicago University Press, 1982), 273–306

RI 'Right of Inspection' (with Marie-Françoise Plissart), trans. David Wills, *Art & Text*, 32 (autumn 1989), 20–97

S *Signéponge/Signsponge*, trans. Richard Rand (New York: Columbia University Press, 1984)

SEC 'Signature Event Context', trans. Samuel Weber and Jeffrey Mehlman, in *Limited Inc* (Evanston, Illinois: Northwestern University Press, 1988), 1–23

Send 'Sendoffs', trans. Thomas Pepper, in *Yale French Studies*, 77 (1990), 7–43.

Sh 'Shibboleth', trans. Joshua Wilner, in *Midrash and Literature*, eds. Geoffrey H. Hartman and Sanford Budick (New Haven: Yale University Press, 1986), 307–47

SOR 'Sending: On Representation', trans. Peter and Mary Ann Caws, *Social Research*, 49:2 (1982), 294–326

Sp *Spurs: Nietzsche's Styles/Eperons: Les Styles de Nietzsche*, trans. Barbara Harlow (Chicago: Chicago University Press, 1979)

SP *Speech and Phenomena and Other Essays on Husserl's Theory of Signs*, trans. David Allison (Evanston, Illinois: Northwestern University Press, 1973)

SST 'Some Statements and Truisms about Neologisms, Newisms, Postisms, Parasitisms, and other Small Seismisms', trans. Anne Tomiche, in *The States of 'Theory': History, Art and Critical Discourse*, ed. David Carroll (New York: Columbia University Press, 1990), 63–95

T 'Telepathy', trans. Nicholas Royle, *Oxford Literary Review*, 10 (1988), 3–41

TP *The Truth in Painting*, trans. Geoff Bennington and Ian McLeod (Chicago: Chicago University Press, 1987)

TPB 'Theory of the Parasite: Bootleg Jacques Derrida', *Blast*, 2 (1990), 16–21

TSICL 'This Strange Institution Called Literature', trans. Geoffrey Bennington and Rachel Bowlby, in *Acts of Literature*, ed. Derek Attridge (London and New York: Routledge, 1992), 33–75

TTP 'The Time of a Thesis: Punctuations', trans. Kathleen McLaughlin, in *Philosophy in France Today*, ed. Alan Montefiore (Cambridge: Cambridge University Press, 1983), 34–50

UG 'Ulysses Gramophone: Hear Say Yes in Joyce', trans. Tina Kendall and Shari Benstock in *Acts of Literature*, ed. Derek Attridge (London and New York: Routledge, 1992), 256–309

v ii   'voice ii', trans. Verena Conley, *Boundary 2*, 12:2 (1984), 76–93

WB   'Women in the Beehive: A Seminar with Jacques Derrida', in *Men in Feminism*, eds Alice Jardine and Paul Smith (London and New York: Methuen, 1987), 189–203

Abbreviations of other works

Chambers   The Chambers Dictionary (Edinburgh: Chambers Harrap, 1993)

JD i   Geoffrey Bennington, 'Derridabase', trans. Bennington, in *Jacques Derrida* (Chicago: Chicago University Press, 1993)

OED   The Oxford English Dictionary, 2nd edn, prepared by J. A. Simpson and E. S. C. Weiner, 20 vols (Oxford: Clarendon Press, 1989)

PFL   Sigmund Freud, *Pelican Freud Library*, trans. James Strachey, Alix Strachey, Alan Tyson, eds James Strachey, Angela Richards, Alan Tyson, Albert Dickson, 15 vols (Harmondsworth: Penguin, 1973–86)

1

Introduction

There is a way of thinking about truth which is not reassuring.

WB, 203

Jacques Derrida's work is *irrational* and *nihilistic*. Derrida is *a charlatan* who offers *little more than semi-intelligible attacks upon the values of reason, truth and scholarship*. This last bit is a quotation from the notorious letter from 'Professor Barry Smith and others', published in the London *Times* on Saturday 9 May 1992 and part of the so-called Derrida affair, concerning the question of whether Derrida was to be or not to be given an honorary degree at the University of Cambridge. Views were expressed both inside and outside Cambridge itself; a University Senate House vote was cast in his favour and, in June 1992, the honorary degree was duly awarded. The affair was significant because — at least in relation to the British media — Jacques Derrida was for the first time being made an object of national curiosity. The 'irrational' and 'nihilistic' labels were bandied about then, had been before and no doubt will be again. As I suggest in the final chapter of this book, such labellings are chiefly a consequence of the fact that those doing the bandying about have not read Derrida's work. The energy or allergy of affirmation with which Derrida's work is charged engages not the irrational but rather another kind of thinking. His work is concerned with 'possibilities that arise at the outer limits of the authority and the power of the principle of reason' (PR, 14). It is concerned with a kind of thinking that tries to reckon with the fact that 'reason is only one species of thought' (PR, 16) — without, for all that, simply valorising the irrational since 'irrationalism, like nihilism, is a posture that is completely symmetrical to, thus dependent upon, the principle of reason' (PR, 14–15).[1] *After Derrida*, then, attempts close readings with a view to elaborating the general

proposition that his work has to do with what he refers to as
'a new *affirmation*, and new ways of taking responsibility' (PR,
15), and indeed with something like a new enlightenment.[2]

Does this mean that I am going to be offering a homage
to Jacques Derrida, that this book presents the work of a
disciple, a labour of filial piety? Take another look at the
photograph opposite. What do you suppose?

How should the title, 'After Derrida', be understood?
Everything might be seen to collapse into these two words
and the ways in which — taken separately or together — they
resist being read, demand to be reread, read still. The readings
traced in the following pages work with at least three senses
of 'after', each of them necessarily problematic: (1) 'after'
Derrida as 'later in time than' Derrida; (2) 'after Derrida' as
'in the manner of', 'in agreement with', 'in honour of' and
even 'in imitation of' Derrida, hence 'after Derrida' as a contemporary version of something like 'after Rembrandt'; and
(3) 'after' Derrida in the sense of 'going in search of' Derrida.
Allow me to make a few brief remarks about each of these
senses of 'after' and about the kinds of issues I shall be
attempting to explore in this book.

Sense (1): It will no doubt seem fairly obvious that the
essays in the present book were written later in time, at a
later date, than the texts by Derrida to which they refer.[3]
These essays come *after* Derrida and indeed focus on questions about the theory and/or practice of history and historiography, literature and literary theory, psychoanalysis and
philosophy, for example, *in the wake of* Derrida's work. But *at
the same time*, to think, write or read 'after' Derrida is to
engage, above all, with how his work affects, contorts, deconstructs the temporal sense of 'after' *as* 'later in time'. In its
readings of philosophical and non-philosophical texts, his
work has been relentlessly concerned with questions of temporality, with what is meant by 'the past', 'the present', 'the
future', 'before' and 'after'. To read or write 'after Derrida'
it is necessary to acknowledge a disruptive series of 'after'
effects — not least in relation to Derrida's deconstructive
readings of 'history' conceived as linear, teleological and esch-
atological, and his exploration of a logic of after-effect or

Alfred Gescheidt, 'Father and Son'
© 1980 Alfred Gescheidt; reproduced by permission

après coup irreducible to a concept of time construed as 'a succession of "befores", "nows" [and] "afters" ' (Aft, 198).

Sense (2): *After Derrida* seeks to provide rigorous expositions of a number of Derrida's writings, concerns and arguments. In this respect the readings advanced here are 'in the manner of', 'in agreement with', 'in honour of' and even 'in imitation of' Derrida's work. But *at the same time* there are differences. These differences could be phrased in terms of an essential paradoxy in the notion of exposition. Reading is inaugural and every exposition, however accurate or faithful, necessarily differs from that which it expounds. Any exposition of a text is necessarily a transposition, a translation and transformation inseparable from invention. Moreover exposition is not secondary. Rather, like a translation, exposition is that which is demanded by the so-called 'original' text. The original is determined and defined by a demand that it be translated or expounded.[4] According to this logic the exposition, conventionally conceived as supplementary, is at the origin.[5] The differences could also be phrased in terms of a notion of rendition. If *After Derrida* presents a number of renditions of Derrida, this entails a sense of rendering not only as representing, reciting or reproducing, but also as translating and thus transforming. 'Rendition' carries an apposite sense of *performance* as well — though, as I hope this study will make clear, the notion of performance here is necessarily paradoxical, *played with*, haunted. As the logic of exposition, rendition or translation may already indicate, what is offered as 'after Derrida' is thus in some sense *beside* and even *before* Derrida. All of this is linked, then, to the problematics of sense (1), 'after' as 'later in time'.

Finally, and inextricably entangled with the foregoing senses, to think 'after Derrida' is to engage with the word 'after' in sense (3), *viz.* the sense of 'going in search of'. Here 'after' suggests that 'Derrida' is not prior or in the past but rather in the future, still to be read, still to come. Moreover, 'Derrida' will perhaps never be reached or discovered. For to be 'after Derrida' is not to be pursuing some attainable goal, quarry or telos but to try to read, write or think in ways which are — as I shall attempt to demonstrate — structurally linked both to mourning and ghosts and to what Derrida calls 'the opening of the future itself' (Aft, 200).

This is a book about or after Derrida, then, in which 'Derrida' is analysed not only as the name designating a series of extraordinary texts which (I would argue) transform the ways in which we might think about history, politics, art and so on, but also as the name designating a remarkable and prolonged meditation on the name itself, and on everything relating to it (the proper, the singular, the signature, the idiom, etc.). *After Derrida* attempts to explore questions of how this meditation identifies 'Derrida' as (to borrow a phrase from *Of Grammatology*) 'the name of a problem' (*OG*, 99) — a problem, or set of problems, concerning identity and authority in general. In the final analysis, this is a book about 'Derrida' as the name of a ghost.

And what about the photograph, Alfred Gescheidt's 'Father and Son'? This picture can in turn perhaps be seen to testify to Derrida's assertion, in a text entitled *Lecture de droit de regards* (translated as 'Right of Inspection'), that 'The spectral is the essence of photography' (RI, 34). Disgusting, disturbing, uncanny, ridiculous, profound, hilarious, monstrous, pathetic, phalloid, castrated, etc., this photograph is, of course, not a photograph in any simple sense.[6] And yet precisely because of this, it transmits certain truths about the nature and order of photography. In the manner of or *after* 'Right of Inspection', then, we could say that this picture or photo-montage illustrates Derrida's suggestion that photography presents 'a different temporality, the so-called "time-lessness of the unconscious"' (RI, 42). What we encounter here is a kind of 'metaphotographic' (73) scenario or event which, in combining at least two photographs, exposes the strange truth in the light of which, 'as always in photography, the scene reproduces itself' (RI, 34). One could say that every photograph involves a kind of 'phantasmimesis' (RI, 84) or that every photograph is in principle framed by the possibility of being a photograph of a photograph.

But photography is not so much about a *suspension* of reference. Rather, as Derrida puts it: 'In the final analysis, however perverse or ingenious the montage might be, [photography] is unable to *produce or domesticate* its referent' (RI,

90, emphasis added). Derrida elaborates on Barthes's claim
that 'in Photography I can never deny that *the thing has been
here*',[7] in order to explore rather the sense that photography
'indefinitely defers a certain type of reality, that of the *percep-
tible* referent' (RI, 91). If 'Father and Son' exemplifies Derrida's
speculation that the 'abyssal inclusion of photographs within
photographs takes something away from looking' (RI, 27), this
peculiar effacement of the gaze motions towards a thought of
the completely other. Barthes argues that, unlike photography, 'Discourse combines signs which have referents . . . but
these referents can be and are most often "chimeras".'[8] For
Derrida, on the other hand, photography is not ultimately
separable from the chimera. He writes:

> where the referent is itself framed within the photographic
> frames, the index of the completely other, however marked it
> may be, nonetheless makes reference endlessly refer. The notion
> of the chimera is then admissible. If there is an art in photog-
> raphy (beyond that of determined genres, and thus in an almost
> transcendental space), it is here. Not that it suspends reference,
> but that it indefinitely defers a certain type of reality, that of the
> *perceptible* referent. It gives the prerogative to the other, opens
> the infinite uncertainty of a relation to the completely other, a
> relation without relation. (RI, 91)

'Father and Son' transmits, perhaps, some apprehension of
this 'infinite uncertainty'. If it is chimerical it is multiply so: it
is not only the chimera of an 'idle or wild fancy' (*Chambers*)
but figures a kind of abyss of the chimera itself, like an abyssal
chimeristic engineering of 'a picture or representation of an
animal having its parts made up of various animals'
(*Chambers*). 'Father and Son' is an undecidably multiple montage (even, or perhaps especially, if it were taken to be *not a
montage at all*): it is, in Derrida's phrase, a 'phantasmaphoto-
graph' (RI, 84). It 'does not suspend its explicit dependence on
a visible referent' (90) but — in its chimericality and in its
darkly exposing the inability for a photograph 'to produce or
domesticate its referent' — it refers to the spectral. To suggest, as Derrida does, that photography is a ghostly *medium*
(RI, 34) is also to start towards the thought that the referent
'itself' is spectralised. In keeping with the concerns of the

following pages, then, Gescheidt's picture casts the shadow of an infinite uncertainty, the light of an uncanny, illimitable reversibility on what Derrida calls 'the retina of time' (RI, 65). It transforms the logic of who or what comes 'before', 'after' or 'at the same time', and *appears* — precisely as an apparition — to embody a claim that Derrida makes himself *in* photography, in the film *Ghost Dance*, namely that 'the future belongs to ghosts, and . . . modern image technology, cinema, telecommunications, etc., are only increasing the power of ghosts'.[9]

After Derrida is among other things, then, a ghost-book, a book about the power of ghosts and about the sort of relationless relation which is at work everywhere, starting out from the title-phrase 'after Derrida' and from the picture with which that title entertains what is at once the most extraneous and most intimate rapport.

A brief summary of the chapters that follow may be helpful. As will perhaps be evident from the chapter titles, my purpose, broadly speaking, is to expound, elaborate, move on from Derrida's work in relation to various topics, including history and historiography, literature and literary criticism, psychoanalysis, philosophy and institutions.

Chapter 2, 'Writing history: from new historicism to deconstruction', offers a re-reading of Derrida's reading of Rousseau in *Of Grammatology* specifically in terms of the notion of surprise. By drawing on the poetry of Les Murray and Maggie O'Sullivan and an entry in a Coleridge notebook, I argue for a reconsideration of the place of surprise in Derrida's work and for its importance as a means of understanding why new historicism is, in effect, not 'new' at all and why Derrida's work remains crucial for thinking about history and historiography in general. As part of the 'revisionist' reading of new historicism implied here I also engage with a brief comparison between Derrida and Foucault — in particular on the notion of the apocalyptic — and suggest some of the respects in which the new historicist appropriation of Foucault can be seen to have been radically partial and reductive.

Chapter 3, 'On literary criticism: writing in reserve', is concerned with the institution of literary studies and the future of literary criticism. Focusing on the work of Geoffrey Hartman, and in particular his book *Saving the Text: Litera-*

ture / Derrida / Philosophy (1981), this chapter sketches a critical re-reading of the initial 'reception' of Derrida's work in the Anglophone world of literary studies. Hartman's account of Derrida is highly idiosyncratic but also in certain important respects characteristic of what came to be known as Yale School or American deconstruction. Tracing a path that includes a reading of Wordsworth's 'The Solitary Reaper', together with an exposition of the deconstructive logic of the pun, 'Writing in reserve' argues the case — after Hartman and after Derrida — for a radically 'amateur', deconstructive theory and practice of literary critical writing, in the form of what I call a hydrapoetics or critico-glossolalia.

Chapters 4 and 5 are concerned with the remains of psychoanalysis. While a number of Derrida's writings could be described as deconstructive accounts of psychoanalytic theory and of (in at least a double sense) the *subject* of psychoanalysis, it is also clear that Derrida is deeply committed to the *preservation* of psychoanalysis (in whatever forms this may take). As he intimates with the title of a recent text: 'Let Us Not Forget — Psychoanalysis' (LUNFP). In particular it may be said that notions of preservation and (not) forgetting are as central to the concerns of deconstruction as to those of psychoanalysis: for any attempt to write, read or think *after Derrida*, the question of psychoanalysis is uncircumventable. These two chapters on 'The remains of psychoanalysis' are at once linked and quite different from one another. They are linked, first of all, by the fact that they investigate two aspects of Freudian psychoanalysis customarily considered marginal, though judged by Freud himself to be the most perplexing two themes with which he was ever preoccupied: first, the question of occultism or more specifically of telepathy; second, the so-called Bacon–Shakespeare controversy (who was 'Shakespeare'?). I consider these themes as the 'unanalysed remainders' or *remains* of Freudian psychoanalysis and suggest ways in which they may be regarded as engaging the *future* of psychoanalysis.

Chapter 4, then, focuses on the question of telepathy and takes off from Derrida's work on this topic. It offers a reading of Derrida's 'Telepathy' (T) both in relation to Freud's writings on the topic and in relation to a theory and practice of literature. The starting-point for my analysis is, perhaps somewhat surprisingly, the notion of laughter: I attempt to elucidate some of the reasons why Derrida should (quite rightly in many respects) be regarded as — in Richard Rorty's phrase — 'a great comic writer', and to delve into the question of the place of laughter in his work. 'Telepathy' is a tremendously funny text, as well as challenging and disturbing: partly what makes it so funny, I suggest, is the way in which Derrida, while writing about Freud's writings on telepathy, takes on Freud's identity, writing *as* Freud and, in particular, telepathetically occupying Freud's thoughts and feelings. Derrida thus presents a fragmentary but at moments hilarious transcription of Freud's thoughts about psychoanalysis and telepathy, only some of which he may be imagined as having really had. Derrida's text does not deal specifically with the question of literature in this context, but I contend that what is being demonstrated here is in fact a theory and practice of fictional writing, specifically as regards that of the omniscient (i.e. telepathic) narrator. This is not to suggest that Derrida's work — or Freud's writings on telepathy — simply fall into the category of 'literature' (whatever that might mean). Rather I propose that, read alongside other contemporary theorists (especially Nicolas Abraham and Maria Torok) and novelists (Toni Morrison, Salman Rushdie and Dennis Cooper), Freud's and Derrida's work on telepathy broaches a quite different notion and practice of writing.

Chapter 5 involves something else again. While Derrida has discussed or referred to the notion of telepathy in various texts (and not only the text entitled 'Telepathy'), he has not — so far as I am aware — devoted specific attention to that other topic which so perplexed Freud, namely the Bacon–Shakespeare controversy. In this chapter, however, I turn to other aspects of Derrida's work. In particular I draw on his various accounts of the notions of proper name and signature — especially in the essay *Signéponge/Signsponge* (*S*) — in an attempt to unfold new ways of thinking (1) about the Bacon–Shakespeare controversy itself; (2) about how we might read some of the works traditionally ascribed to Shakespeare (in particular *Hamlet*, *Romeo and Juliet*, *Antony and Cleopatra* and *The Tempest*); (3) about the institution of psychoanalysis and its relations to 'literature'; and finally (4) about the proper names of Freud and Derrida 'themselves'.

Chapter 6, 'Philosophy and the ruins of deconstruction', is an essay or experiment engaged with figurations of love and ruin in Derrida's work. As elsewhere in *After Derrida*, what is going on is the attempt to provide a *rendition* of *how* Derrida's work performs (polyphonously, interruptively, telepathetically) as much as of *what* it says, argues, describes. It is a matter of trying to render what is at once 'literary' *and* 'philosophical' in Derrida's work, or rather what might be going on in the wake of their mutual contamination, as regards both 'form' and 'content'. 'Philosophy and the ruins of deconstruction' accordingly proceeds by exploring the notion and practice of the fragment and aphorism in Derrida's writing. In fragmentary and aphoristic fashion it then seeks to make sense of Derrida's claim (here being read necessarily out of context, as a fragment) that all of his work can be referred back to Heraclitus, and thus to consider the relations between deconstruction and the origins of western philosophy. This leads on to some thoughts about ruins in relation to drawing, painting and poetry: I move from Derrida's essay on self-portrait drawing (*MB*) to reflect on some of the most astonishing self-portrait paintings of the twentieth century, those of Helene Schjerfbeck, and then to a reading of Wallace Stevens's 'A Postcard from the Volcano' in terms of the self-portrait, ruins and what Derrida defines (in Che) as the poetic or 'poematic'. I conclude with a fragmentary anecdote and a fragment of an unpublished Derrida letter.

Chapter 7, 'Foreign Body: "The deconstruction of a pedagogical institution and all that it implies" ', brings into focus one of the recurrent preoccupations of the book as a whole, that is to say the notion of foreign body. As I suggest in earlier chapters, for example, deconstruction can be considered as a kind of foreign body within new historicism; the 'distractions' of telepathy and the Bacon–Shakespeare controversy constitute foreign bodies within the conceptual framework of psychoanalysis; and in fact the very project, interjection or *intra*jection of *After Derrida* as a whole involves a kind of foreign-body inhabiting of Derrida's work. As exposition, rendition or countersignature, indeed, *After Derrida* can be conceived as in some sense always already *within* Derrida's writing. Chapter 7 ranges over some of the ways in which we might conceive the *import* of the notion of foreign body — for instance in terms of a theory of tradition and influence and in terms of the relations between deconstruction and parasitism — but the primary aim is to consider how Derrida's thought might be put to work within the institution of the university and, most specifically, to ponder the question of how Derrida's work on institutions — and especially the institution of the International College of Philosophy — might be addressed within the localised context of a particular research group and seminar based within a particular university. What happens if one envisages a seminar, a research group or research body called, precisely, Foreign Body?

Chapter 8, 'On not reading: Derrida and Beckett', reflects on various senses of 'not reading' in relation to Derrida's work, including (1) the paradox whereby a writer's work can produce effects without being read, (2) the relations between deconstruction and the unread or unreadable, and (3) the possible interest and significance of Derrida's professed inability to write about the work of Samuel Beckett, that is to say his enigmatic confession to having ' "avoided" [Beckett] as though I had always already read him and understood him too well' (TSICL, 61). This final chapter considers the correspondingly enigmatic question of writing and thinking not only after Derrida but also after Beckett. It concludes with a theory and practice of *excitation*.

Notes

1 As regards the imputation of charlatanism, let us here merely recall a consistent and explicit aim of all Derrida's writing, succinctly expressed for example in 'Limited Inc', *viz.* 'I do not seek to establish any kind of authenticity' (LI, 55). In other words it is precisely the point of his work to show that nothing is purely authentic: inauthenticity, forgery, charlatanism and so on are always possible and indeed constitute a necessary possibility inscribed in the very structure of the allegedly authentic. Derrida seeks to highlight a law of necessary but *undecidable* contamination at work in every attempt to distinguish between the authentic and non-authentic, pure and impure, charlatan and non-charlatan. I return to the ques-

tion of this kind of contamination in my discussion of the 'amateur'
and 'professional', in Chapter 3.

2 For Derrida's discussion of the term 'new enlightenment', see for
example LI, 141; PR, 5, 19; IDCN, 75; and, more generally, *The Other
Heading (OH)*.

3 Actually, even this 'fairly obvious' point would need to be qualified,
since some of the book — for instance, Chapter 5 — was 'originally'
published (though later revised) *before* some of the Derrida texts
to which it refers.

4 I consider the disseminatory effects of 'exposition' at greater length
in an essay entitled 'Expositioning', in *Afterwords*, ed. Nicholas Royle
(Tampere: Outside Books, 1992), 19–42.

5 The difference might also be phrased in terms of the logic of signature and countersignature, as it is by Geoffrey Bennington when he
notes: 'if the signature (Plato's, for example, but also Derrida's, of
course) calls for our countersignature, this call and our reply to it
are not necessarily situated in (filial or other) piety, supposing that
we know what such piety would be outside the play of signatures'
(*JD i*, 164). Bennington here points to an alterity inscribing every
filiation: 'the play of signatures' or 'iterability' in some sense precedes every relation, makes possible every signature-event while
also dislocating or ex-propriating it.

6 On the phalloid and castrated, we may recall Freud's notion that a
multiplication of phallic images (the baldness, the cigarettes) signifies castration: see Sigmund Freud, 'Medusa's Head', *Standard Edition
of the Complete Psychological Works of Sigmund Freud*, trans. James
Strachey, vol. XVIII (London: Hogarth Press, 1955), 273. Cf. also
Derrida's contention, in 'Right of Inspection', that 'Sexual difference
has been interfered with by photographing photographs' (43). One
could say that if Gescheidt's picture figures the obliteration of
maternity, it also obliterates the figure of the father as such.

7 Roland Barthes, *Camera Lucida: Reflections on Photography*, trans.
Richard Howard (London: Fontana, 1984), 76; cited by Derrida, RI, 90.

8 *Camera Lucida*, 76; cited by Derrida, RI, 90.

9 Cited in Bennington and Derrida's *Jacques Derrida (JD i / ii)*, 349.
See also Maud Ellmann's fine essay 'The Ghosts of *Ulysses*', in *The
Languages of Joyce*, eds R. M. Bollettieri Bosinelli, C. Marengo Vaglio
and C. Van Boheemen (Amsterdam and Philadelphia: John Benjamins, 1992), 103–19. Ellmann's essay begins with this scenario: 'In the
recent film *Ghost Dance*, directed by Ken MacMullen, Jacques
Derrida is interviewed by an etherial young woman who asks him
if he believes in ghosts. "That's a hard question," he smiles,
"because, you see, I am a ghost" ' (103).

2

Writing history: from new historicism to deconstruction

> In both field and forest, as in ponds, rivers, and oceans, gastropods are an important part of the decomposer community.
>
> *Encyclopaedia Britannica*

> ... if there will have been a surprise and therefore an event ...
>
> (*JD ii*, 140)

In his book *White Mythologies: Writing History and the West*, Robert Young claims that Derrida 'has not been concerned to formulate a new philosophy of history'.[1] While this is no doubt true (the very phrase 'a new philosophy' sounds distinctly unlike Derrida), it is clear that the implications of his work for historiography in general are quite massive. In question here is everything that is brought together under Derrida's rubric of the notion of history as the history of meaning. In this chapter I will attempt to explore in particular what might be understood by the phrase 'writing history', specifically in so far as this may in turn help to clarify the relationship between new historicism and deconstruction. I propose to do this by trying to follow apparently quite separate tracks: the first, in the form of a kind of entrée, has to do with molluscs, the second is a reading of Derrida's *Of Grammatology* (*OG*). This will lead, in turn, to a consideration of the apocalyptic, in so far as this relates to the work of Derrida and Foucault. I will then conclude with some remarks about new historicism and deconstruction, and about writing history *after Derrida*.

i. Molluscs

To start off, then, I would like to cite two pieces of poetry, ornamenting or supplementing them with as brief a commentary as possible. The first is a poem by Les Murray, entitled 'Mollusc':

By its nobship sailing upside down,
by its inner sexes, by the crystalline
pimplings of its skirts, by the sucked-on
lifelong kiss of its toppling motion,
by the viscose optics now extruded
now wizened instantaneously, by the
ridges grating up a food-path, by
the pop shell in its nick of dry,
by excretion, the earthworm coils, the glibbing
by the gilt slipway, and by pointing
perhaps as far back into time as
ahead, a shore being folded interior,
by boiling on salt, by coming uncut over
a razor's edge, by hiding the Oligocene
underleaf may this and every snail sense
itself ornament the weave of presence.[2]

In keeping with many of Murray's other poems, 'Mollusc' is explicitly concerned with the question of anthropomorphism. Are we capable of a non-anthropomorphic conception of, for example, an emu, or a mollusc?[3] Is there anything besides what he calls, in a poem of that title, 'anthropomorphics'?[4] 'Mollusc' is engaged with disturbances of temporality — with a molluscous logic of 'pointing / perhaps as far back into time as / ahead' — and evokes the necessary but perhaps impossible notion of a non-anthropocentric history. This is suggested most of all in the cryptic invocation of the Oligocene period which this 'mollusc' (both the 'subject' of the poem and, as the title authorises us to suppose, the poem as such) hides 'underleaf'.[5] 'Oligocene' (it may be recalled) refers to certain Tertiary strata belonging to the intermediate era between the Eocene and Miocene, in other words to a period between roughly thirty-seven and twenty-three million years ago. The word comes from the Greek *oligo*, 'little, few', and *kainos*, 'new'. 'Oligocene', then, specifically refers to the sparseness of the number of 'fossil molluscs of living species' (*Chambers*). The mollusc, in short, defines the Oligocene and determines history. But the otherness of this history and historicity must remain hidden 'underleaf', as the fiction of a nominal (oligocenic) time that was never present, inassimilable to any historicity or historicisation on the basis of a so-

TAB. XX.

GENESIS Cap. I. v. 21.
Opus quintæ Diei.

I. Buch Moſis Cap. I. v. 21.
Fünfftes Tagwerck.

The work of the fifth day: the creation of molluscs. Plate from J.-J.
Scheuchzer's *Physique sacrée ou histoire-naturelle de la Bible*, 1732

By permission of the Trustees of the National Library of Scotland called human living present. 'Mollusc' is a poem about itself ('may this and every snail sense . . .') and reminds us that poetry in general, as for example in the Arab Dream in Words-worth's *The Prelude* (Book V), has been powerfully figured in molluscous terms, specifically as a shell.[6] It may remind us also that the word 'mollusc' is from the Latin *molluscus*, 'soft-ish', *mollis*, 'soft', and would thus correlate in suggestive ways with Derrida's theorisation of the poem as a hedgehog, in the essay 'Che cos'è la poesia?' (Che). Like the hedgehog, the mollusc is oddly vulnerable, being hard outside but soft inside; with the additional peculiarity, however, that the mol-lusc (at least in Murray's poem) seems also to figure a general disorientation of what is the right way up ('By its nobship sailing upside down'), and of what is 'extruded' and what is 'folded interior'. But if the word 'itself' is crucial to the final line of Murray's poem and if the poem does indeed call to be read as self-reflexive or meta-poetic, it is also other than this: the poem suggests the weaving logic of an ornamentation or supplementation which cannot perhaps finally be assimilated or reassimilated within an anthropomorphic or anthropo-centric notion of 'sense' or 'presence'.

The second poem is less than a poem, more a poematic extract, comprising a few lines, rather violently excised from Maggie O'Sullivan's extraordinary poem, entitled *States of Emergency* (1986):

> caged mollusc — cracked out in
> thistled bangling liver toxic
> cannibal quicklies —
> pluck vision[7]

Far more than Murray's poem, these lines seem to me to resist commentary. One could attempt to analyse the uncertainly comic surrealism of the phrase 'caged mollusc' or 'cannibal quicklies', or attempt to engage with the ab-ject evocation of the cracking out of what — like the definition of the *Unheim-lich* which Freud borrows from Schelling — 'ought to have remained . . . secret and hidden but has come to light'.[8] One might try to explore what is intimated as cannibalistic here as the uncanny contamination of the mollusc and human, highlighted by the eco-logic that what may have been caged by humans also cages them in turn: the toxification of the planet is the toxification of the human. But I would like to leave these lines to trail across these pages, leaving their tracks as traces or reminders of what (after O'Sullivan) I propose to call states of emergency, irreducible to sense or presence, a molluscous poisoning of identity, a cracking out of the inside, the plucking of vision or blinking of an eye in which history *bangles*. To bangle here would be not only to 'flap' or 'hang loosely' (like the skirts of a mollusc) but also to 'fritter away' (*OED*). History happens in no time. I would like to suggest that, more than any other kind of writing perhaps, poetry promotes an apprehension of that surprise or astonishment about which Derrida writes in relation to language and history, *viz.* 'astonishment by language as the origin of history' (FS, 4) and surprise as the condition of possibility of any rigorous historiography.[9]

ii. Back to Grammatology

I want to explore the notion of surprise in Derrida's account of writing and history, especially in his reading of Rousseau in *Of Grammatology*, in an attempt to elucidate some rather fleeting remarks about new historicism made in a more recent text, entitled 'Some Statements and Truisms about Neologisms, Newisms, Postisms, Parasitisms, and Other Small Seismisms' (SST) (1990). He here argues that every 'species', every movement, every *ism*, in so far as it can be said to be *one* (to have unity and specificity), 'constitutes its identity only by incorporating other identities — by contamination, parasitism, grafts, organ transplants, incorporation, etc.' (66). The logic of the supplement, with which we may by now like to believe we are familiar, works at the heart of every identity. Thus Derrida claims that

> new historicism introjects while denying it, incorporates without admitting it, a *concern with* history which . . . was already active, present and fundamental, for example, in the very poststructuralism which the supporters and promoters of new historicism think it is absolutely crucial to oppose. (68)

Linked to this, Derrida also asserts that 'the problematic of

the border and of framing — that is, of context — is seriously
missing in new historicism' (92–3). What is being suggested
here is that poststructuralism or, more specifically perhaps,
deconstruction constitutes a foreign body within new historicist writing. Deconstruction involves precisely the concern
with history which new historicists claim it lacks. Moreover
this failure or elision on the part of new historicists might be
most readily illustrated in terms of the question of *context*.

In rather snail-like fashion, then, I wish to move across a
few pages of *Of Grammatology* — a book which, published in
1967, we may sometimes like to suppose we left behind years
ago[10] — in order to try to elaborate an assertion made by
Geoffrey Bennington: 'deconstruction, insofar as it insists on
the necessary non-coincidence of the present with itself, is in
fact . . . the most historical of discourses imaginable'.[11]

Deconstruction happens in no time.

Of Grammatology is, as Derrida put it in a recent interview,
'a history book through and through' (TSICL, 54). It argues
'that reading should free itself, at least in its axis, from the
classical categories of history — not only from the categories
of the history of ideas and the history of literature but also,
and perhaps above all, from the categories of the history of
philosophy' (*OG*, lxxxix). As he states in the Exergue, this
involves the attempt to show that 'the history of truth, of the
truth of truth, has always been . . . the debasement of writing,
and its repression outside "full" speech' (*OG*, 3). In *Of Grammatology*, as elsewhere, Derrida views history as unavoidably
a metaphysical concept to the extent that it is always 'determined in the last analysis as the history of meaning' (*P*, 49)
and in so far as it is 'not only linked to linearity, but to an
entire system of implications (teleology, eschatology, elevat-
ing and interiorizing accumulation of meaning, a certain type
of traditionality, a certain concept of continuity, of truth, etc.)'
(*P*, 57). *Of Grammatology* is concerned to show, however, that
a certain notion of *writing* is the condition of possibility of
history — 'writing opens the field of history' (27), as Derrida
puts it — and thus to explore the ways in which it is possible
to glimpse the *closure* of that 'historico-metaphysical epoch'
which he calls 'logocentrism' (*OG*, 4).

Let us focus, then, on that section of *Of Grammatology* ('... That Dangerous Supplement...') in which Derrida is seeking to provide 'a justification of [his] principles of reading' (158) and an explanation in particular of what might be 'exorbitant' in his reading of Rousseau. Central to '... That Dangerous Supplement...' is the question of history. Derrida is concerned to show how Rousseau's work allows for the identification of 'a decisive articulation of the logocentric epoch' (162). This has to do with the singular manner in which Rousseau's work belongs to the logocentric epoch, with how it 'repeats the inaugural movement' (98) (a movement at work from Plato to Descartes and beyond), whereby writing is construed as secondary or supplementary to speech. This belonging, argues Derrida, is also a non-belonging or ex-propriation: the repetition is also a difference. For Rousseau 'starts from a new model of presence: the subject's self-presence within *consciousness* or *feeling*' (98). Rousseau's work allows Derrida to gesture towards 'the point of a certain exteriority in relation to the totality of the age of logocentrism' (161). It permits the broaching of 'a certain deconstruction of that totality', a gesture which is 'subject to a certain historical necessity' (162) but which at the same time implies a rethinking or reinscription of the historical as such; in particular it engages with a notion of writing that would be the condition of possibility for history itself.

Of Grammatology works with at least two senses of the term 'writing'. Derrida's special notion of writing as the condition of possibility of history itself should not be confused with, but neither can it be easily dissociated from, a recognition that history is radically determined by writing, by what, in the conventional sense, is *written*.[12] It is in this context for example that Derrida proposes, in the Preface to *Of Grammatology*, that 'The age already in the *past* is in fact constituted in every respect as a *text*' (lxxxix). But 'writing' and 'text', as he elaborates these terms, are not restricted to their conventional senses. Rather, he wishes to show how these terms are necessarily subject to what he elsewhere calls 'unbounded generalization' (TTP, 40). To say that history is radically determined by writing, then, is to say that it is constituted by a general or unbounded logic of traces and remains — general and unbounded because these traces and remains, this work of remainders and remnants, are themselves neither presences nor origins: rather, they too are constituted by traces and remains in turn. Such a formulation of 'writing' may seem at variance with the immediacy of speech and 'the subject's self-presence within *consciousness* or *feeling*', for that immediacy seems indeed constantly to be effacing itself. Derrida's argument, however, is that speech and the experience of self-presence are themselves only possible on the basis of a logic of writing, that is of repetition and difference, of traces and remains. 'Writing' then is not simply (as Rousseau phrases it) a 'supplement to the spoken word' (cited *OG*, 7): as mark, trace, spacing, it inhabits speech (and the very experience of self-presence) as its condition of possibility, while at the same time being nowhere either present or absent.

Derrida's reading of Rousseau elaborates a logic of supplementarity which is at once described and unstated in Rousseau's work, which both is and is not within 'the metaphysical orb' (162). As Derrida puts it: 'The supplement itself is quite exorbitant, in every sense of the word' (163). A reading (Derrida's of Rousseau) will inevitably be a matter of tracing *and* adding to what has been written. Reading is snail-like and supplementary, we could say, but it is not simply a question of repeating what Rousseau (or Derrida) has said. To read or write *after Derrida* it is not possible merely to repeat. It cannot be a matter of 'reproducing, by the effaced and respectful doubling of commentary, the conscious, voluntary, intentional relationship that the writer institutes in his exchanges with the history to which he belongs thanks to the element of language' (158). Yet such 'doubling commentary' itself is necessary, Derrida suggests: it should have a place in any 'critical reading'. This notion of reading and critical procedure, it may be remarked, has no relation whatsoever to the 'non-historical', 'anti-historical', 'purely subjective', 'anarchistic' kinds of slogans brandished against Derrida by his would-be detractors. As Derrida's text goes on to state: 'Without this recognition and this respect, critical production would risk developing in any direction at all and authorise itself to say almost anything. But this indispensable guardrail has always only *protected*, it has never *opened* a reading' (*OG*, 158).

Of Grammatology, then, and '...That Dangerous Supplement...' in particular, can be said to dramatise a moment of surprise, the opening or evocation of a supplementarity that would be exorbitant. To *open* a reading, in this context, would seem to be a matter of being precisely *apprehended*, a matter of being *taken by surprise*. Derrida, then, is concerned with a notion of writing that *haunts* speech, a kind of ghost-writing that likewise haunts the *being* of the writer and takes by surprise any writing that s/he may produce, as well as any writing (or reading) that might be produced in response to that writing. This, then, would be the drama or theatre of surprise and it constitutes, Derrida suggests, a kind of necessary starting-point: '*We should begin* [my emphasis] by taking rigorous account of this *being held within* [*prise*] or this *surprise*: the writer writes *in* a language and *in* a logic whose proper system, laws, and life his discourse by definition cannot dominate absolutely. He uses them only by letting himself, after a fashion and up to a point, be governed by the system' (158).

iii. Grammatology for beginners

Where should we begin? Derrida answers: '*Wherever we are*: in a text *already* [my emphasis] where we believe ourselves to be' (162, tr. mod.) [*Quelque part où nous sommes: en un texte déjà où nous croyons être*].[13] This syntactically enigmatic supposition of the 'already' (are we in a text before we believe or in some sense as an effect of believing?) situates the mad law of the supplement, the surprising law of historicity, the states of emergency out of which 'history' calls to be thought. It illustrates the 'axial proposition' that 'there is nothing outside the text' (163), in other words there is nothing outside context (even though, or rather precisely because, context is non-saturable). As a number of commentators have noted, this is not to suggest that everything is textual, that everything can be treated as text, as happening in a book or on a computer-screen. Rather, there is nothing exempt from *effects* of textuality.[14] 'The referent is in the text' (19), as Derrida puts

it in the interview on 'Deconstruction in America' (DA) in
1985. His concern is to elaborate readings which take rigorous
account of the ways in which any text (in the traditional sense
of that word) and any writer (the notion of the writer being
itself 'a logocentric product' (DA, 16)) are variously affected,
inscribed and governed by a logic of text, of supplementarity
or contextualisation, which can never be saturated or
arrested. Every text (in the traditional sense of that term) has
meaning only on the basis of belonging to a supplementary
and 'indefinitely multiplied structure' (*OG*, 163) of contextualisation and incessant recontextualisation. As Derrida declares,
towards the end of Part II of *Of Grammatology*: 'The supplement is always the supplement of a supplement. One
wishes to go back *from the supplement to the source*: one must
recognize that there is *a supplement at the source*' (304).

To be astonished 'by language as the origin of history'
(FS, 4) is first of all, then, to acknowledge that this origin is
multiple, divided in itself, ghosted.[15] Language, text and writing are constituted by supplementarity, by a network of traces
and referrals, references to other references, a generalised
referribility without simple origin, presence or destination.
It is because Derrida is concerned with how this logic of
interminable, ghostly referribility at once situates and dislocates every text, every speech act, and indeed *experience* in
general, that he is able to claim, as he does in 'Deconstruction
in America', that what he is doing in his own writings is
'more referential than most discourses that [he] call[s] into
question' (DA, 20).

'We should begin', 'we must begin' (162) [*il faut com-
mencer*: 233]: there is an obligation (what here and at numerous other moments Derrida refers to as an *il faut*)[16] to take
rigorous account of this logic or structure of being surprised.
It is in its failure to reckon with this structure of surprise
that we might in part understand Derrida's criticism of new
historicism as taking insufficient account of the problematic
of *context* — the context, that is to say, in the first instance,
of the writer writing. The notoriously misunderstood proposition that 'There is nothing outside the text' may be more
helpfully phrased as 'There is nothing outside context' (see,
for example, LI, 136, and BIO, 873) — but only on condition

of trying to situate an experience of context as necessarily in excess of, supplementary to and breaking with any experience, presence or intention. The writer is 'taken by surprise' (160) — the writer here being 'The philosopher, the chronicler, the theoretician in general, and at the limit everyone writing' (160). 'The person writing is inscribed in a determined textual system' (160). Thus the crucial significance, for Derrida, of the notion of the supplement is that its 'resources' should be 'sufficiently *surprising*' that 'the presumed subject' who says (or writes) ' "supplement" ' will always be saying 'more, less, or something other than what he *would mean* [*voudrait dire*]' (157–8).

This logic would apply to Derrida in turn. Any impulse to take hold of, or to surprise, the figure of Derrida-the-writer must be checked or surprised in turn by that which, in the logic of the supplement, has always already apprehended and carried this figure away. This is the law of writing (and of reading). *Of Grammatology* makes this clear when it describes the 'doubling commentary' that should have a place in any 'critical reading'. Derrida remarks:

> if reading must not be content with doubling the text, it cannot legitimately transgress the text toward something other than it, toward a referent (a reality that is metaphysical, historical, psychobiographical, etc.) or toward a signified outside the text whose content could take place, could have taken place outside of language, that is to say, in the sense that we give here to that word, outside of writing in general. (158)

The law is surprising ('it cannot legitimately transgress . . .') in so far as it concerns the radical disturbance of the referent (Derrida, me, you, history). If there is a writerly, written or writable 'I', in other words, it belongs to a writing that is nowhere present: an impossible, unpresentable 'I', then, an 'I' which could be described as 'literary' or 'fictional' but only if these terms are understood in the most disruptive and dispossessing sense. It would no longer be a question of a notion of literature that would be opposed to, for example, 'the real' or 'history', nor would it be a question of a notion of the fictional that would be opposed to, for example, 'the factual' or 'the true'. Rather it would be the hypothesis of a radically 'literary' *and* radically 'historical' (because 'written' but unthinkable, unpresentable) dislocation of every 'I', wherever it presents itself, whether in a so-called work of literature, philosophy, literary theory, or historiography, etc.

Suffice to say, the most fundamental assumptions and characteristics of new historicist writing are here called into question: that is, not only the characteristic tendency (as H. Aram Veeser has suggested) whereby the individual 'desires and interests' of new historicists 'openly preside' in their writing, but also what Frank Lentricchia refers to as the new historicist belief in 'the autonomy of self-fashioning' as such.[17] Even Stephen Greenblatt's comparatively modest contention, at the end of his essay 'Toward a Poetics of Culture', that 'methodological self-consciousness is one of the distinguishing marks of the new historicism in cultural studies as opposed to a historicism based upon faith in the transparency of signs and interpretative procedures' falters here.[18] The problems surrounding an implicit privileging of a notion of critical and professional 'self-consciousness' are compounded by that of methodology; for the notion of the 'methodological' itself is fraught with questionable assumptions concerning teleology, instrumentalism and the authority of the human agent who would use or apply such a 'method' or 'methodology'.

iv. Foucault after Derrida

One way of thinking about new historicism and seeking to demonstrate the kinds of exclusions which characterise it (including, for example, the specific forms of its 'methodological self-consciousness') would be to re-examine its relation to the work of Michel Foucault. Let us at least briefly sketch out a possible trajectory or *jetty* for such a re-examination.[19] At stake here would be the notion of reading Foucault after Derrida, including the task of trying to reckon with what is paradoxical or, precisely, unreadable in that phrase. 'Foucault after Derrida' would concern not only the ways in which Foucault's work might be read in the wake of Derrida's, and how Derrida's work affects a reading of Foucault (in other words, a relatively conventional sense according to which, historically, Derrida's work calls to be thought about as coming *after* Foucault and as being influenced by and indebted to Foucault's example, both as a writer and as a teacher)[20] but also the implications of the sense that, conversely perhaps, Foucault comes after, not before, Derrida.[21]

Foucault's work is generally taken to be the basic and informing force behind new historicism, and in particular his work in the late 1970s and early 1980s, when he was teaching at Berkeley. The 'final' Foucault, that is to say, the Foucault of 'technologies and care of the self', has been crucial for the self-fashioning of new historicism. But one can argue that there is another reading of Foucault, or other readings, that radically dislocate the most intimate concerns of new historicism, fundamentally disrupting its criteria of 'methodological self-consciousness' and the subject-centred, identity-oriented forms of its politics. Such readings would follow Foucault's proposal in *The Archaeology of Knowledge*, namely to analyse history in terms of a

> discontinuity that no teleology would reduce in advance; to map it in a dispersion that no pre-established horizon would embrace; to allow it to be deployed in an anonymity on which no transcendental constitution would impose the form of the subject; to open it up to a temporality that would not promise the return of any dawn.[22]

This is a Foucault of radical heterogeneity, of an essential disabling of self-identity and reflexivity. It is the sort of Foucault who writes deliriously, professing neither exactly in his own voice nor in the voice of Nietzsche, 'Nothing in man — not even his body — is sufficiently stable to serve as the basis for self-recognition or for understanding other men'; and (in the same essay) 'the purpose of history, guided by genealogy, is not to discover the roots of our identity but to commit itself to its dissipation'.[23]

No doubt Derrida is in some respects closer to this Nietzschean–Foucauldian position than to that of new historicism. Professing history, for Foucault and for Derrida, has to do with the adoption of an apocalyptic tone. Both are concerned with the notion of the 'end' or 'ends of man', with a 'discontinuity that no teleology would reduce in advance' and 'a dispersion that no pre-established horizon would embrace'. This concern is explicitly, meticulously historical: to say that Foucault's famous envisioning of the end of man in the Conclusion to *The Order of Things*[24] and Derrida's meditation in 'The Ends of Man' (EM) belong to the particular kind of apocalypticism of Paris in the latter part of the 1960s is not the basis — as some have hastened to suppose — for classifying Foucault's or Derrida's work as in some way 'merely' representative or reflective of its time. Can a work, even for example in the supposedly minimal form of a signature, ever be this? The logic of iterability that founds the very possibility of a signature, its very readability, would suggest otherwise. Not for nothing, then, does Derrida subscribe the date (12 May 1968) below the last words of 'The Ends of Man' (EM, 136). The specificity and singularity of the date, like that of Derrida's signature, is crucial: it is, for Derrida, the implacable stipulation of the time of writing, a decisive specification of the 'wherever we are' (*OG*, 162). As he puts it elsewhere, 'To date is to sign' (*EO*, 11).[25] Derrida's work, then, insists on this specificity and singularity of the time and place of a production, of a text and of a reading. This historical specificity is matched by the careful attention to the historical specificity of the texts he reads: thus in *Of Grammatology*, for example, considerable energy is devoted to the (in some respects highly 'traditional') question of assessing *when* Rousseau's *Essay on the Origin of Languages* might have been written.[26] *At the same time*, however, Derrida's work is concerned with a deconstruction of classical notions of history, extending indeed to the exorbitant thought of the deconstruction of meaning as such (in so far, that is to say, as 'history' is construed as 'the history of meaning'). As we have seen, one way in which such a deconstruction might be figured is in terms of the logic of the supplement, the argument that the origin is always multiple, or that the supplement is at the origin but there is always another supplement (supplementarity is 'indefinitely multiplied' as Derrida puts it). In other words, *Of Grammatology* gestures towards 'the play of history — as supplementarity' (*OG*, 179).

There are differences between Derrida's apocalypticism, however, and Foucault's. Derrida's work does not very easily fit in with Foucault's proposed deployment of historical analysis 'in an anonymity on which no transcendental constitution would impose the form of the subject'. The affirmation of anonymity, for example, is not strikingly 'Derridean'.[27] While Foucault's work could be said to aspire to an insistent posing of the Beckettian question 'what does it matter who's speaking?',[28] Derrida's style is rather to *invoke* the ostensible singularity and propriety of names and signatures, if only to exhibit their simultaneous decomposition. It may also be said that, in comparison with Foucault, Derrida has provided a much more sustained analysis of the very notion of the apocalyptic, for instance in such essays as 'The Ends of Man' (EM), 'Living On: Border Lines' (LO/BL), 'Of an Apocalyptic Tone Recently Adopted in Philosophy' (AT), 'No Apocalypse, Not Now' (NA) and *Cinders* (C), as well as in longer texts including *Glas* (*G*) and the 'Envois' (E) section of *The Post Card*. If Derrida and Foucault share an intense preoccupation with the critique and active disordering of a classical concept of history (and all its corollaries: linearity, teleology, presence, the subject and ideology), it is Derrida who has meditated most explicitly on the apocalyptic *per se*. To think about 'Foucault after Derrida' is to engage with the force and effects of this meditation.

v. Apocalypse how

Professing history has to do with the adoption of an apocalyptic tone, with states of emergency. We can hear this throughout Derrida's writings, for example in the kind of proclamation about 'text' and 'history' that he makes in 'Living On': a *text*, he announces,

> is henceforth no longer a finished corpus of writing, some content enclosed in a book or its margins, but a differential network, a fabric of traces referring endlessly to something other than itself, to other differential traces. Thus the text overruns all the limits assigned to it so far (not submerging or drowning them in an undifferentiated homogeneity, but rather making them more complex, dividing and multiplying strokes and lines) — all the limits, everything that was to be set up in opposition to writing (speech, life, the world, the real, history, and what not, every

field of reference — to body or mind, conscious or unconscious, politics, economics, and so forth). (LO, 84)

Working through this language of presence and immediacy ('henceforth') and of totalisation ('all the limits', 'everything', 'every field of reference'), 'Living On' *takes on* the sort of apocalypticism evoked by Maurice Blanchot's words, 'The end is beginning'.[29] As Derrida notes elsewhere: 'The end is beginning, signifies the apocalyptic tone' (AT, 24).

If 'Of an Apocalyptic Tone' is among Derrida's most exhilarating, most delirious meditations, this is in part because it gives such a breathtaking performance of the apocalyptic multiplicity of voice within every voice. Breath is surprised before the voice, the voice that says 'Come': the tone of this 'Come' 'is the disorder or the delirium of destination (*Bestimmung*), but also the possibility of all emission' (24). 'Come' is apocalyptic but this 'come' is always still to come (in French, *àvenir*: also, 'the future'). If it is the nearest that thought can come to death, it is also perhaps, by the same token, the nearest it can come to presence. The 'to come' of 'come' corresponds to the logic whereby a letter can always not arrive at its destination and consequently this necessary possibility of non-arrival (this *destinerrance*) is inscribed within the structure of every dispatch, so that no letter ever completely arrives. This haunting non-arrival, which is not simply a negativity, is the condition of possibility of every 'arrival'. The 'come' is still coming, still to come. 'Come' comes from the other, it is multiple and traverses: it belongs to no present. One cannot say *what* this 'Come' *is*, Derrida suggests, 'because the question "what is" belongs to a space (ontology, and from it the knowledge of grammar, linguistics, semantics, and so on) opened by a "come" come from the other' (34). This is in part why an apocalyptic tone, in the terms in which Derrida elaborates it, can only ever be *adopted* or taken on — and even here it would be necessary to stress that this adoption is not the work of any adoption *agency*: the apocalyptic here traverses, inscribes, adopts multiplicity, divisions, alterity within *itself*. Adoption without identifiable adopter or adoptee, then. Or as Derrida puts it, effectively echoing the Foucauldian and Beckettian motif noted above, 'as soon as one no longer knows who speaks or who writes, the text becomes apocalyptic' (AT, 27). The apocalyptic and *affirmative* 'Come' which Derrida seeks to invoke is a kind of figure for the condition of possibility (and impossibility) of self-presence, including the presence-to-oneself of one's own voice. As he notes elsewhere: 'To hear oneself is the most normal and the most impossible experience' (QQ, 297). The apocalypticism of 'come', then, becomes exemplary of the structure of experience in general: 'wouldn't the apocalyptic be a transcendental condition of all discourse,' asks Derrida, 'of all experience even, of every mark or every trace?' (27). To which one should perhaps add that this 'transcendental' is more precisely a kind of 'quasi-transcendental', concerning at once the condition of possibility and impossibility of 'all experience'.

If new historicism can be seen to have involved variously reductive readings of Foucault's work (not to mention Derrida's), it becomes particularly important — in the context of any rigorous attempt to read Foucault after Derrida — both to try to render or countersign the Nietzschean and Beckettian apocalypticism of his work and, at the same time, to acknowledge Derrida's crucial inflection of that apocalypticism. That is to say, it is necessary to take account of the notion that Derrida's work is both apocalyptic and a deconstructing of the apocalyptic. In response to critics who have been curious or suspicious of the fact that he has '*taken on* an apocalyptic tone and put forward apocalyptic themes' (AT, 30), he insists on a series of qualifications, *viz.*:

> That I have multiplied the distinctions between closure and end, that I was aware of speaking of discourses *on* the end rather than announcing the end, that I intended to analyse a genre rather than practise it, and even when I would practise it, to do so with this ironic genre clause wherein I tried to show that this clause never belonged to the genre itself. . . . (30)

If, as he goes on to suggest, 'all language on apocalypse is also apocalyptic and cannot be excluded from its object' (30), this participation does not efface the 'ironic' and simultaneous force of non-belonging. This interruption is a kind of apocalypse of the apocalypse, and it is in this context that

Derrida is concerned with asking: 'to what ends?' To what
ends do people wish to come, 'who declare the end of this or
that, of man or the subject, of consciousness, of history, of
the West or of literature' (23)? Professing history has to do
with clarity and lucidity, with the apocalyptic desire for the
deconstruction of apocalyptic discourse itself:

> We cannot and we must not — this is a law and a destiny —
> forgo the *Aufklärung*, in other words, what imposes itself as the
> enigmatic desire for vigilance, for the lucid vigil [*veille*], for
> elucidation, for critique and truth, but for a truth that at the
> same time keeps within itself some apocalyptic desire, this time
> as desire for clarity and revelation, in order to demystify or, if
> you prefer, to deconstruct apocalyptic discourse itself and with
> it everything that speculates on vision, the imminence of the
> end, theophany, parousia, the last judgment. (22)[30]

No apocalypse, not now, as the title of another Derrida essay
(NA) has it. Or, as might be said, without question mark:
apocalypse how.

vi. Surprising history

No supplemental asylum, then, no place of refuge from the
ceaselessly doubling, dislocating power of the supplement.
What we have instead are states of emergency, states which
would be apocalyptic but at the same time a deconstruction
of the apocalyptic. Not *a* state, but *states*: there is no singular.
'Emergency' here would involve not only the sense of 'A situation, esp. of danger or conflict, that arises unexpectedly and
requires urgent action', but also the sense of 'The process of
emerging into view' (*OED*), like a snail's head emerging from
its shell. History comprises states of emergency; but there
can be no history, and therefore no states of emergency, without that which surprises and deconstructs every emergence,
the emergence of every 'I' and the emergence of every event.

For if a notion of surprise is, as I have been trying to
suggest, central to Derrida's argument in his reading of Rousseau, it will be necessary to try to take account of how the
thought of surprise is itself displaced, apprehended, to be
read *otherwise* in Derrida's work. To illustrate this we might

consider a remark made by Coleridge in a notebook entry in 1802: 'October 3 — Night — My dreams uncommonly illustrative of the non-existence of Surprize in sleep'.[31] There are various ways in which Coleridge's remark might be read. Principally one can read it as something he jotted down, sometime after waking up, either during the night of 3 October or the next morning, a note making the observation that in one's dreams surprise is non-existent. Such a truth would accord with the otherwise perhaps superfluous supposition that, in order to be taken by surprise, it is necessary to be in such a condition that surprise is possible. Here surprise is being figured, as it were, starting out from the opposition of dream and wakefulness and more specifically from a privileging of the latter. This privileging is implicit in the fact that we have already assumed Coleridge's notebook entry to have been made retrospectively and from a state of wakefulness. Coleridge, we assume, was awake when he wrote these words, and this assumption seems to be reinforced, in effect, by the word 'uncommonly' which — to the extent that it suggests precisely *surprise* (the uncommon as the surprising) — underlines the apparent legitimacy of the paradigmatic opposition that would put dream and the non-existence of surprise on one side, and wakefulness and a potential capacity or readiness for surprise on the other. But we might also point towards the unsettling of such a reading — an unsettling, perhaps, that would (along with much of Coleridge's poetry in fact) query the notion of a purely non-somnambulistic subject, that would ponder the temporal oddity of the cited extract (the vague yet ominous generality of the word 'Night', the absence of any verb), and that would dislocate any simple presupposition of appropriation or ownership (implied by the phrase 'My dreams').[32]

Such possibilities would perhaps comport with some of the questions with which Derrida concludes *Of Grammatology*: 'The opposition of dream to wakefulness, is not that a representation of metaphysics as well? And what should dream or writing be if, as we know now, one may dream while writing? And if the scene of dream is always a scene of writing?' (315–16). More generally, we could say that Derrida is concerned with a notion of *surprise* that would itself be deconstructive, a notion of surprise which would be — as he puts it in the early essay 'Force and Signification' — 'incomparable to any other, a surprise responsible for the articulation of what is called Western thought' (FS, 4). *Of Grammatology* may thus be seen as tracing a notion of *surprise* that would no longer be governed by the logic of agency figured by 'Derrida' or 'Rousseau' ('the writer'), or by the opposition of dream and wakefulness, in other words a notion of surprise as the surprise of the other, 'a certain experience of the impossible' (to adopt what is perhaps Derrida's most condensed definition of deconstruction)[33] that would be the invention or surprise of the impossible, the impossible surprise perhaps of never waking up, of the dream of a completely other sleep (to draw on the words of *Antony and Cleopatra*). Here — but in the most vigilant fashion — Derrida's text becomes (and simultaneously ceases to be) apocalyptic. It broaches a hypnopoetics, in the blinking of an eye, in the extruded wizening of a glance or 'pluck vision'.

vii. Envoi

By way of concluding this historical envoi, I would like (if a bit provocatively) to say a little more in justification of the subtitle of this chapter, 'from new historicism to deconstruction'. The provocation would consist in adopting a rhetorical ploy that can be seen as crucial to the coherence of new historicist writing, *viz.* referring to poststructuralism or deconstruction as a kind of unified movement or phenomenon and doing so in the past tense.[34] New historicism is a thing of the past. As Derrida notes in 'Some Statements and Truisms', the imposition of each newism or postism — whether 'new historicism' or 'poststructuralism' — is 'basically the same gesture, the cultural stratagem as an inevitable by-product of the oldest of historicisms' (68). The failures or limits of new historicism involved an unwillingness or rather perhaps a structural inability to acknowledge the foreign body of deconstruction. The deconstructive notion of surprise I have sought to trace here is a long way from the proclaimed concerns of new historicists. The measure of this distance is the measure also of how new historicism merely repeated, with whatever

pretence of disruption or change, a figuration of history as
'the history of meaning' — subject-centred, identity-oriented
and, above all, anthropocentric. No time for the molluscous.

In this chapter I have sought to unfold some of the implications of Derrida's work in relation to the question of history
and historiography, and to sketch a kind of re-thinking of
the relations between deconstruction and new historicism,
especially in so far as the latter might once have been thought
to come 'after' the former.[35] Specifically as regards new historicism, the challenge of Derrida's work remains unanswered:
this is partly because comparatively little attention has so far
been given to his contention that there is nothing essentially
human about language — that the track or trace is in a sense
as much molluscous as human — and because comparatively
little attention has been given to the notion that history, like
deconstruction, is less about the past than about the opening
of the future. Writing history has to do with states of emergency, states given both to an acknowledgement that 'The
future can only be anticipated in the form of an absolute
danger' (*OG*, 5) and to a recognition that the past was never
present.[36]

Notes

1 Robert Young, *White Mythologies: Writing History and the West*
(London: Routledge, 1990), 64. *White Mythologies* is an admirable
study of the importance of Derrida's work in relation to what can
loosely be referred to as modern and postmodern historiography.
Young, however, imposes a particular kind of constraint on Derrida's
work in this context. This is announced at the end of Chapter 4
of his book where he writes: 'Having elaborated the paradoxical
conditions of historicity, of any history or totalization, Derrida himself has been particularly concerned to analyse those such as Husserl, Heidegger or Levinas, who have been involved in investigations
of time and temporality. Although it would be possible to pursue
the question of history in terms of such analyses of the forms of
historicity, such an enquiry would take us on a very different path
from that prompted by our original question, namely if poststructuralism can apparently be faulted by reference to a history which it
neglects, where in Marxism can this history be found?' (67). The
present study could be said to differ from Young's work in that it
attempts to explore 'investigations of time and temporality' in a

slightly less circumscribed manner. In particular we are concerned with issues of voice, performativity and style which, on one level at least, may appear to fall outside the scope of Young's work, though it would also be fair to say that *White Mythologies* does not lack the apocalyptic tenor, for example, which we are here interested in analysing. Such apocalypticism is evident for instance in what is doubtless one of the most provoking sentences in Young's book, in which he suggests that 'today at the end of the twentieth century, as "History" gives way to the "Postmodern", we are witnessing the dissolution of "the West" ' (20).

2 Les Murray, *Translations from the Natural World* (Paddington, NSW: Isabella Press, 1992), 26.

3 On the emu in particular, see 'Second Essay on Interest: the Emu', in Les Murray, *Collected Poems* (Manchester: Carcanet, 1991), 205–7. The anthropomorphism of its opening lines, for instance, is at once comical and troubling: 'Weathered blond as a grass tree, a huge Beatles haircut / raises an alert periscope and stares out / over scrub . . .' (205).

4 See *Collected Poems*, 173. In this poem, for example, we encounter such characteristically odd, seemingly throwaway lines as: 'Hunting, we know, is mostly a form of shopping / where the problem's to make the packages hold still.' It is not at all clear how far we are being invited to affirm the value of such 'anthropomorphics'.

5 Cf. the apostrophe to the emu in 'Second Essay on Interest': 'Are you Early or Late, in the history of birds / which doesn't exist and is deeply ancient?' (206)

6 William Wordsworth, *The Prelude, 1799, 1805, 1850*, eds. Jonathan Wordsworth, M. H. Abrams and Stephen Gill (New York: Norton, 1979). Among many other examples of poems 'about' molluscs, one might think of Francis Ponge's 'Le Mollusque', which focuses on the mollusc's lifelong dwelling indoors (as it were), before comparing this with the human: 'Rien à faire pour l'en tirer vivant. / La moindre cellule du corps de l'homme tient ainsi, et avec cette force, à la parole, — et réciproquement.' (Francis Ponge, *Le Parti pris des choses*, ed. Ian Higgins (London: Athlone Press, 1979), 48.) This appears in English in Francis Ponge, *Things: Selected Writings*, trans. Cid Corman (Fredonia, New York: White Pine Press, 1986), as: 'No way to pull it out alive. / The least cell of the human body clings so, and with this force, to speech, — and reciprocally' (22).

7 Maggie O'Sullivan, *States of Emergency* (Oxford: International Concrete Poetry Archive Publication no.11, 1986).

8 See Sigmund Freud, 'The "Uncanny" ', in *PFL* 14: 345.

9 For two recent accounts of the notion of surprise, see Timothy

Clark, 'By Heart: A Reading of Derrida's "Che cos'è la poesia?"
through Keats and Celan', *Oxford Literary Review*, 15 (1993), 43–80;
and Sarah Wood, 'Surprise in Literature', *Angelaki*, 1:1 (1993), 58–68.
Clark invokes the notion of surprise as a means of defining the
poetic, as follows: 'The poetic obviously does not constitute the
addressee in his or her empirical being. Rather it reconfigures identity as the experience of surprising the I in the mode of having
become the addressee projected by the text and as having, unfore-
seen, entered what Celan calls the other's time, that is the singular
temporality "here", "now", of the text in its multiple singularity. It
interrupts, or cuts across, subjectivity conceived as a structure of
possible self-return' (67–8). Similarly, Wood is concerned in her
essay 'to undo the magic isolation of surprise as the property of
somebody, or as an aesthetic effect which merely blinds and binds
the movement of writing' (60).

10 In this sense, of course, there is no going *back* to it: cf. Bennington's
contention that 'The event constituted by the reading of Rousseau
in the *Grammatology*, for example, did not take place in 1967 only
later to become absorbed into familiarity, but comprises an essential, persisting *Unheimlichkeit*' (*JD* i, 252).

11 Geoffrey Bennington, 'Demanding History', in *Post-Structuralism and
the Question of History*, eds Derek Attridge, Geoff Bennington and
Robert Young (Cambridge: Cambridge University Press, 1987), 17.

12 For a recent and wide-ranging account of 'writing' in the work of
Derrida, see Christopher Johnson, *System and Writing in the Philosophy of Jacques Derrida* (Cambridge: Cambridge University Press,
1993).

13 *De la grammatologie* (Paris: Minuit, 1967), 233. Further page references to the 'original' French edition will be given within square
brackets in the main body of the text.

14 Cf. Bill Readings's account of this aspect of Derrida's work in 'The
Deconstruction of Politics', in *Reading de Man Reading*, eds Wlad
Godzich and Lindsay Waters (Minneapolis: University of Minnesota
Press, 1989), 228.

15 Cf. Geoff Bennington and Robert Young who, in their Introduction
to *Post-Structuralism and the Question of History*, assert that this
origin 'is no origin at all' (8).

16 It may be helpful to note here the emphasis that Derrida at the
same time gives to *il faut* in the sense of 'lack'. See, for instance,
PSAWV: ' "Il faut" does not only mean it is necessary, but, in French,
etymologically, "it lacks" or "is wanting". The lack or lapse is never
far away' (315). The 'il faut' is among other things, then, a double-
bind and — in so far as it might be anthropomorphised as gifted

with speech — speaks to an obligation or acknowledgement that is
at once necessary and impossible.

17 See H. Aram Veeser's Introduction to *The New Historicism*, ed. Veeser
(London and New York: Routledge, 1989), xi. Frank Lentricchia's
essay in the same volume, 'Foucault's Legacy: A New Historicism?'
(231–42), attacks new historicism and the work of Stephen Greenblatt in particular as being 'a continuous narrative whose source
and end is "myself". Lentricchia goes on: 'Greenblatt's "myself" is
representative, it finds its home in "we", and "we" is nothing other
than the community of disappointed liberal middle-class literary
intellectuals — and how many of us really stand outside this
class? — whose basic need is to believe in the autonomy of self-
fashioning' (238). Even in the launching of the attack, however, with
its in many ways crazily rhetorical question ('How many of us really
stand outside this class?'), Lentricchia seems unable to avoid this
including himself. The term 'self-fashioning' of course primarily
recalls Greenblatt's *Renaissance Self-Fashioning: From More to Shakespeare* (Chicago: University of Chicago Press, 1980). In so far as it
may seem reasonable to take Greenblatt's book as illustrative of
new historicist concerns, it may be remarked that it is pervaded
with assumptions of a kind that Derrida's work calls into question.
Self-representation occurs, it is assured, no matter how supposedly
'textualized' its figuration. Self-fashioning can be counted on, as a
kind of permanent fashion: its aetiology, its modes and manifestations may vary radically, for instance in the period of western
history since the Renaissance, but there is little apparent disturbance as regards the coherence of the concept of self-fashioning as
such, a coherence predicated on a logic of the self-identity of self
and of the very process of fashioning. In this way it is inextricably
bound up with certain fundamental presuppositions about distinctions between 'literature' and 'social life'. For instance in the following short passage: 'And with representation we return to literature,
or rather we may grasp that self-fashioning derives its interest precisely from the fact that it functions without regard for a sharp
distinction between literature and social life. It invariably crosses
the boundaries between the creation of literary characters, the
shaping of one's own identity, the experience of being molded by
forces outside one's control, the attempt to fashion other selves'
(*Renaissance Self-Fashioning*, 3). I would suggest that this passage
is characteristic, for example, in the sense that, while it invokes
the idea of a crossing of boundaries, and thus implies a kind of
contamination of the literary and non-literary, it is in fact by this
very gesture reinstating the principles of coherence governing 'the
creation of literary characters', the autonomy of a notion of 'one's
own identity', and so on.

18 See Greenblatt, 'Toward a Poetics of Culture', in Veeser, 12.

19 'Jetty' is a term which Derrida works with in 'Some Statements and Truisms' and which he defines as 'the force of that *movement* which is not *subject, project,* or *object,* not even rejection, but in which takes place any production and any determination, which finds its possibility in the jetty' (SST, 65).

20 See, for example, Derrida's comments on his gratitude to Foucault as a teacher, in 'Cogito and the History of Madness', in *Writing and Difference*, trans. Alan Bass (London: Routledge and Kegan Paul, 1978), 31.

21 To elaborate a rigorous account of 'Foucault after Derrida', in other words, would entail a deconstructive reading of the very conventions of intellectual history, linearity, legacy, debt and influence. Such a task is in part the project of Herman Rapaport's study *Heidegger and Derrida: Reflections on Time and Language* (Lincoln: Nebraska University Press, 1989). For a review article which offers a careful exploration and critique of this aspect of Rapaport's book, see Timothy Clark, 'Inventions of Intellectual History', in *Afterwords*, ed. Nicholas Royle (Tampere: Outside Books, 1992), 124–33.

22 Michel Foucault, *The Archaeology of Knowledge*, trans. A. M. Sheridan Smith (London: Tavistock, 1972), 203.

23 Michel Foucault, 'Nietzsche, Genealogy, History', in *Language, Counter-Memory, Practice: Selected Essays and Interviews*, trans. Donald F. Bouchard and Sherry Simon, ed. Bouchard (Oxford: Blackwell, 1977), 153, 162.

24 Michel Foucault, *The Order of Things: An Archaeology of the Human Sciences* (London: Tavistock, 1970), 386–7.

25 For a more extended account of dating in relation to signature and singularity, see the remarkable essay 'Shibboleth' (Sh).

26 See *OG*, 170ff.

27 This is of course in many ways an overgeneralisation: *The Post Card*, for instance, is pervasively concerned with the force of anonymity. And the very fact that it has seemed appropriate here to put the word 'Derridean' in scare quotes may further caution against too clear-cut a sense of how, in the light of Derrida's (and Foucault's) work, we might think about the anonymous. I return elsewhere to the question of Derrida, the authorial name and anonymity, below.

28 See Michel Foucault, 'What Is an Author?' in *Language, Counter-Memory, Practice*, 115, 138.

29 See *La Folie du Jour / The Madness of the Day*, trans. Lydia Davis (Barrytown, New York: Station Hill), 10.

30 Cf. too Derrida's remarks on the importance of trying 'to remain faithful to the ideal of the Enlightenment, the *Aufklärung*, the *Illuminismo*, while yet acknowledging its limits', in *OH*, 79.

31 *The Notebooks of Samuel Taylor Coleridge*, vol.I (1794–1804), ed. Kathleen Coburn (London: Routledge and Kegan Paul, 1957): 1250.

32 Such an unsettling might start, in fact, with the bizarre way in which the Notebook entry itself goes on: 'October 3 — Night — My dreams uncommonly illustrative of the non-existence of Surprize in sleep — I dreamt that I was asleep [!!] in the Cloyster of Christs Hospital . . .'.

33 See, for example, PIO, 36, and Aft, 200.

34 See, for example, Catherine Gallagher's 'Marxism and the New Historicism', in Veeser, 37–48. Gallagher writes, and apparently senses no problems in deploying the past tense, as follows: 'What came to be called "deconstruction", then, could be used to confirm important New Left tenets and, at the very time when the movement was losing momentum, to provide an explanation for that loss. Many of us, however, found that we could neither renew our faith in Marxism nor convert to deconstruction, for neither seemed sufficient to explain the permutations of our own historical subjectivities [*sic*] and our relationship to a system of power, which we still imagined as decentered, but which we no longer viewed as easily vulnerable to its own contradictions' (42).

35 My point here is, of course, at least in part polemical: in other respects it would no doubt be necessary to consider the ways in which 'new historicism' is *also* a kind of foreign body within 'deconstruction' or, at any rate, within 'deconstruction*ism*'. Cf. Derrida's comments on this in 'Some Statements and Truisms': 'If deconstructionism were what it is accused of being, and *when* it is and *where* it is formalist, aestheticist, ignorant of reality, of history, enclosed in language, word play, books, literature, indifferent to politics — I would consider Marxism and new historicism absolutely legitimate, necessary, urgent . . . Marxism and new historicism are very different theoretical phenomena . . . Nevertheless they have in common only that their most *significant* present traits come from *within* the space of the deconstructive jetty [or 'deconstruction' as we have been using the term in the present chapter] and consist *in* their marked opposition to stabilizing deconstruction*ism*' (SST, 90).

36 See, for example, *OG*, 66, and cf. Derrida's comments on the work of Paul de Man in *Mémoires*: '. . . one could say that for Paul de Man, great thinker and theorist of memory, there is only memory but, strictly speaking, the past does not exist. It will never have existed in the present, never been present . . .' (*M*, 58–9).

3

On literary criticism: writing in reserve

There is something secret. But it does not conceal itself.

POO, 21

d

Limited ink. This essay might more appropriately have been called Uneasy Pieces. Tentative, fragmentary, it consists of no more than a few provisional speculations or auscultations about literarity, monstrosity, reaping and reserve, intimations of mortality figured otherwise. In particular, the aim is to explore the question of literary criticism after Derrida and to do so by focusing on one of the earliest and most impassioned literary critical accounts of Derrida's work in English, Geoffrey Hartman's *Saving the Text*.[1]

e

Saving the Text: the question of literature, after Hartman and after Derrida. What would it mean to retrieve *Saving the Text*? Or to suppose that its irretrievability is what saves it? 'Writing in reserve' — such is what is apparently given as a title here, but one which might suggest that it is already effaced, that 'writing in reserve' is not a title but rather designates a writing (or reading) — including the writing or reading of the title — which is held back, deferred, in a variety of senses *not presentable*. 'Reserve': from the Latin *re* ('back') and *servare* ('to save'). 'Writing in reserve' will try to ponder the question of the possible force and value of this *re* which comes to remark every saving: a matter, then, of what is at stake in the hypothesis that 'saving the text' is necessarily 're-saving' it, reserving it: 'saving the text' would be impossible without a logic of writing in reserve. 'Writing' as noun and as verb; 'in reserve', held back, preserved, set apart, relied upon; 'reserve' in the sense of what is unexploited, still available, deferred, and even (in an archaic sense) what is 'disguised' or 'secret' (*OED*). Writing in reserve is multiple. It concerns, as I will try to show, the question of literary criticism and a kind of anonymity or pre-anonymity.[2]

f

To talk about writing in reserve is to engage with the thought of a critical glossolalia, a poetico-telephony or computer network operating multiple channels simultaneously. A sort of hydrapoetics, in effect.

g

Including at least three heads, three tongues, three voices, gathered around the following: (1) how Hartman reads Derrida's *Glas* (*G*) in *Saving the Text*; (2) how this reading is more generally characteristic of the early 'reception' of Derrida's work within English-speaking literary culture; and (3) the possibility of what Hartman calls 'a new concept of *reserve*'.

h

Writing in reserve: a hydrapoetics or critico-glossolalia. As simple as abc.

i

But the logo-alphabetical ordering of this abc will already have been disturbed, paragrammed and paragogued in advance, uneasy pieces, disseminating fragments of what Wordsworth calls the 'dream of human life'.[3]

j

Hartman and Derrida then: *Saving the Text: Literature / Derrida / Philosophy* is a 1981 collection of essays, some of which had been published earlier in journals and elsewhere, between 1975 and 1980. On the one hand it is an extremely, even stubbornly singular work, charged with Hartmaniacal wit, anxiety and inventiveness. On the other, it is a suggestive and revealing collection of essays in terms of the so-called reception of *Glas* and of Derrida's work more generally, especially in the US but also in Britain and elsewhere, in the late 1970s and beyond. The dedication at the front of *Saving the Text* — 'For the Subject' (it was never quite clear, at least to me, whether this was supposed to be referring to the human subject or the subject of literary studies or, possibly, on the basis of this ambiguity, the subject of ambiguity itself) — is touched with a sense of its author's own particular brand of apocalyptico-melancholy humour but at the same time encapsulates a more general anxiousness about the implications of Derrida's work for literary studies as a subject and for the subject reading or studying literature. *Saving the Text* offers the first detailed readings of the book which Derrida himself said he 'never thought . . . could . . . be translated' (Pro, 17) and which was not to appear in English until 1986: Hartman's readings (especially 'Monsieur Texte' and 'Epiphony in Echoland', which first appeared in the *Georgia Review* in 1976 and 1977), in their own special way, offer exposition and commentary. Published at around the same time as Gayatri Chakravorty Spivak's translation of *Of Grammatology* in 1976, Hartman's essays help to provide students and teachers of literature with a context for the appreciation and understanding of Derrida's work. *Glas* is held to be Derrida's most demanding, least translatable work: Hartman's essays, so evidently at ease with French and German, light the way to a literary critical appropriation of Derrida's work in the English-speaking world.

k

But at the same time, *Saving the Text* has its own *take* on that work, indeed it is offered as what Hartman calls 'a counterstatement to Derrida' (121). Hartman's 'counterstatement' is, by his own account, less a 'refutation' than 'a different turn': *Saving the Text* is at once a commentary and (to adopt

Derrida's term) a double commentary, commentary with a difference.

1

How might this countering and doubling be attended to, for instance if we try to analyse what could be called the party-line of Wordsworth's voice in Hartman's prose? In question here are the implications and importance of the literary within Hartman's writing. How would a critico-glossolalia or hydrapo-etics affect the notion of Hartman as the Wordsworthian soli-tary reaper of a page? How do we hear Wordsworth today? Where might following the Wordsworth party-line lead us? Keeping an ear out for Wordsworth, let us keep these ques-tions on the line, in reserve.

m

Saving the Text wishes to argue that 'Writing destabilises words, in the sense that it makes us aware . . . of their alien frame of reference' and makes us aware of the fact that words 'come to us already interpreted, trailing clouds of meaning' (xxi-xxii). Hartman's book seeks to explore the importance of an affirmative response to his question: 'is not writing too much with us?' (xx), above all by arguing the case for hearken-ing to what he calls 'the affective power of voice' (xxii). Hart-man is concerned with heart and hurt, with how these are configured in 'that resonating field we call the psyche' (xxii): it is the psychically or affectively wounding (as well as healing) power of words that matters. Hartman writes: 'Semiotic analy-sis of the word in the word, even when as penetrating as Derrida's, with his method of putting statements *en abyme*, cannot reach that field of pathos or power' (xxii). Hartman calls for a new and different attention to the importance of voice, of the (appositely Wordsworthian) 'power of sound', in other words the importance of reading literature as 'an active kind of hearing' (128) — what Yvor Winters for example referred to as 'the audible reading of poetry' or, more recently, Garrett Stewart has theorised as the phonotextual space of 'reading voices'.[4] *Saving the Text* is compelled, for example,

by the occluded if not occult senses of audition, by the hidden
reserves of hearing, as if by the 'Murmuring from Glaramara's
inmost caves'. Hartman calls us to the fascination of 'the
ineluctable ear, its ghostly, cavernous, echoic depth' (123),
and ultimately towards an experience of language which lies,
he says, not only 'too deep for tears but also too deep for
ears' (148).

n

'A new concept of reserve.' *Saving the Text* is in many respects
a book about reserve, about reservation as much as preservation or conservation. Among other things and in a rather
equivocally *reserved* way, it is a book about reserve as the
guiding principle both of a kind of decorum and of a kind of
discursive strategy. Hartman writes:

> Derrida tells literary people only what they have always known
> and repressed. Repressed too much, perhaps. The fullness of
> equivocation in literary structures should now be thought about
> to the point where Joyce's wordplay seems normal and
> Empson's *Seven Types* archaic. A thousand and one nights of
> literary analysis lie before, a Scheherazade to keep an emperor
> awake beyond his intentions. Until a new concept of *reserve*, not
> merely panic or defensive, is developed, one that could result
> in as fine a sense of decorum as literature itself often displays.
> (23)

'Reserve' here suggests 'artistic restraint', 'restrained
manner', 'reticence', even 'aloofness' (*Chambers*). How would
such a notion of reserve be compatible with what Hartman
has more recently praised as the 'public and conversational
mode' of literary criticism, the sort of 'conversationalism' he
associates with the work of Stanley Cavell and Richard Rorty?[5]
Let us propose the following hypothesis: 'a new concept of
reserve', this improbable formulation, would perhaps motion
towards the thought of a writing, at once more uncontrollably
conversational (because constitutively polyphonic) and more
intractably reserved than Hartman himself might seem dis-
posed to acknowledge. Let us approach this hypothesis gradu-
ally, without undue panic or defensiveness.

o

But *Saving the Text* also expresses, or rather intimates, deep
reservations about Derrida's work and about *Glas* in particular. Derrida's style is, for Hartman, at once fascinating and
troubling (xxiv). This ambivalence pervades *Saving the Text*:
if the book is reserved, decorous and admiring of Derrida's
work, it is also quite unreserved, or unreservedly violent, in
its essayed put-downs. I would be tempted — if there were
time in reserve — to digress a little here on the relations
between punning and ambivalence: Derrida, for Hartman, is
an author whose work is difficult if not impossible to put
down.[6] The ambivalence of Hartman's characterisation of
Derrida's work, and of *Glas* in particular, is evident throughout
Saving the Text: Derrida's style is held to be 'as much a problem as the heavier Heidegger' (22); it is 'cold' (72) and
'elegantly humorless' (22), neither 'exotic' nor 'precarious'
(45); it is 'exhibitionistic' (xxv), 'far from beautiful' (85),
'barely readable prose' (86). Linked to this, there is Hartman's
more specific characterisation of Derrida-as-author: he writes
of Derrida's 'disregard for the reader' (72); Derrida is characterised as 'anxious' (61), 'jealous' (75), 'a great amateur of
Littré and Wartburg' (82), someone who 'never misses a trick'
(106).[7]

p

In an apparently unreserved exploitation of the pun, Hartman
describes Derrida as 'a great amateur' — a phrase at once
loving and putdownish: the amateur is *the lover*, but also
someone to be identified with what is 'superficial, trifling,
dilettantish, or inexpert' (*Chambers*). Hartman's own style in
this respect might be compared with Tennyson's — described
in *Saving the Text* as 'so easy, so unlabored — deceptively
"idle" ' (111). If we say that Hartman is a great amateur of
Derrida, no doubt we say so — like Hamlet — with an idle
tongue. Idle for a number of reasons, including at least the
following: (1) Hartman's writing might be seen to open on to
a radical questioning of the relations between the amateur
(the enthusiastic, loving and passionate reader, writer or

thinker) and the professional, an encounter that has to do with contemporary forms of academic professionalism in the humanities (increasing bureaucratisation and 'automatism' of research; the pragmatically desirable but perhaps impossible subsumption of the 'literary' within more broadly 'cultural' studies; the insidious obligations toward a 'jargon of civility').[8] Hartman's writing might in this way provoke us to other ways of thinking about what Samuel Weber has described as 'the limits of professionalism'.[9] (2) Linked to this, it is necessary to stress that *Saving the Text* is, in certain respects at least, history: however maverick, it is in significant ways representative of how Derrida's work was initially 'received' in the English-speaking world, and is thus bound up with the more general impact of deconstruction on current configurations of 'literature', 'literary criticism', 'philosophy', 'cultural studies', etc.

Our reading here is concerned to idle back and forth between a possible displacement and re-mapping of amateur–professional distinctions, on the one hand, and a retrieval and rethinking of the 'reception' of Derrida's work in the English-speaking world on the other. Tracing a logic of what is in reserve, this idle intrigue has to do with what is amateur, with a certain exorbitance in the very condition of passion and love.

q

Let us try to sketch a path towards this deconstructive thinking of *amateurism*. *Saving the Text* admirably helped to make accessible a body of work (*Glas* in particular, but Derrida's oeuvre in general) until then mostly unknown to readers in English. But *Saving the Text* also presented decisive misreadings and misrepresentations of Derrida's work. These misreadings and misrepresentations work not only at the specific level of situating *Glas* as the Derridean equivalent to *Finnegans Wake* (a characterisation that has tended to stick, despite careful critical arguments to the contrary),[10] but also more broadly. First, *Saving the Text* relentlessly characterises Derrida's work in terms of 'indeterminacy', its 'hermeneutics of indeterminacy' (106) and its 'indeterminacy principle'

(98).[11] That this implies a significant misunderstanding may
be suggested by Derrida's own remarks on this topic, in the
1988 'Afterword' to *Limited Inc*, when he distinguishes
between indeterminacy and undecidability and observes: 'I
do not believe I have ever spoken of "indeterminacy", whether
in regard to "meaning" or anything else . . . "deconstruction"
should never lead either to relativism or to any sort of indeter-
minism' (ATED, 148). Second, Hartman represents deconstruction as a 'method' (*Saving the Text*, 7): against this we have
Derrida's repeated characterisations to the contrary, for
instance in 'Letter to a Japanese Friend': 'Deconstruction is
not a method and cannot be transformed into one' (LJF, 273).[12]
Third, Hartman's account of Derrida is undermined by a certain linguisticism. Hartman contends that in Derrida's work
'the whole, dizzying metaphysical desire for presence or
absence' is seen as 'infinitely mediated not only in language
but as language' (18). He accuses Derrida of a kind of 'antimes-
sianic exuberance' about the idea of death as 'already, and
endlessly, in language' (19). Again, this sort of linguisticism is
explicitly rejected by Derrida — most succinctly perhaps in
the interview with Richard Kearney when he talks of deconstruction precisely as a search for 'the "other of language" '
(DO, 123). Linguisticism in this respect can indeed be
regarded as logocentrism *par excellence*.[13] If Hartman is able
to find 'admirable' the extent to which Derrida allows us to
see 'how consistently the human condition is a verbal condition' (104), it is also evident from Hartman's own rhetoric
that his 'me', 'we', 'us' and 'our' occupy a kind of extralinguistic high ground.[14]

　　In fact, this gulf between Hartman and Derrida — or this
fundamental misunderstanding of Derrida's work on Hartman's part — is still apparent in a discussion involving themselves and Wolfgang Iser, which took place in Jerusalem in
August 1986 and was published at the end of that year (DTJ).
Here Derrida seems to be in the company of two interlocutors
who do not or cannot appreciate the basic point that his
work is concerned with a *non-instrumentalist* conception of
language. His emphasis here is quite unequivocal. In response
to a remark from Iser about how Derrida 'use[s] language', he
says that deconstruction is 'a way of writing, it's a way of *not*

using, but being *involved in* the language, and in the difference
between languages, in the different idioms' (DTJ, 6, emphases
added). Similarly Hartman refers to his own abiding convic-
tion that with Derrida's texts 'there is a feeling of tremendous
verbal energy' and that 'one of the satisfactions is in seeing
what you do with language' (emphasis added). Hartman goes
on: 'I can't release myself from the idea that there is a question
of style in you; and that this question of style is very important, that you are influential in literary circles because you
have faced that question of style, and *you work within it*'
(DTJ, 6, emphasis added). Again, Derrida's response entails a
specific rejection of this instrumentalist notion of *using* language (and therefore a rejection of the allied notion of style).
He says:

> I wouldn't call this style. Style usually implies that the writer
> uses a given language with its given possibilities, and leaves
> his mark on the form; whereas what I'm interested in are the
> possibilities within the language to dissociate words, to graft, to
> integrate many languages in one, and to exploit the hidden
> possibilities in the language. (6)

'Hidden possibilities in the language': in other words, perhaps,
writing in reserve. We will come back to this.

Finally, following Derrida, it would be necessary to criti-
cise and dislocate the speech/writing distinction that is so
fundamental to Hartman's own predominating argument in
Saving the Text about the importance of voice, the ear, the
music and sounds of sound. Hartman's claim that 'The rhetoric that interests Derrida derives solely from the specific
power of the *written*' (120) not only reflects a more pervasive
misconception of what Derrida refers to by the paleonym of
'writing',[15] but also elides the attention that Derrida's own
work has consistently given to the importance of voice. That
such attention is bound up with a deconstruction of speech/
writing distinctions does not legitimate Hartman's critical mis-
hearing in this context. Such attention is clear, for example,
in the remarkable essay 'Qual Quelle' (QQ) (1971) with its
eerie tracing of voice in the poetry and other writings of
Valéry, and indeed in the seminal/disseminal essay of 1968,
'Différance', with its specific stress on that uncanny space

'*between* speech and writing, and beyond the tranquil familiarity which links us to one and the other, occasionally reassuring us in our illusion that they are two' (Diff, 5). The years
since the publication of *Saving the Text* have in some ways
borne witness to an even more audible refutation of what
Hartman had categorised as an uncomfortable stress on writing and writerliness in Derrida's work, at the expense of voice
and what Hartman calls 'auscultations' (142). One might think,
for instance, of the astonishing meditation on/of multiple
voices in 'Of an Apocalyptic Tone Recently Adopted in Philosophy' (AT) (given at Cérisy in 1980) or the 1984 essay on
Joyce entitled 'Ulysses Gramophone: Hear Say Yes in Joyce'
with its insistent evocations of what Derrida calls 'the living
yes, archived in the very quick of its voice' (UG, 276).

While Hartman's account of Derrida is highly singular,
then, it is also emblematic of how Derrida's work was — and
in some respects continues to be — misread and misunderstood. If an emphasis on indeterminacy, linguisticism and
writerliness was characteristic of so-called Yale School or
American deconstruction — that is to say, more generally, of
deconstruction as a kind of literary critical method —
Derrida's own formulations of deconstruction (starting perhaps with the claim that deconstruction is never single, but
always multiple, and with the contention that deconstruction
can never be one's 'own', it never belongs to, starts out from
or returns to a self-identical subject) have been extremely
different.

r

Let us focus on one further apparent point of conflict or
difference between Hartman and Derrida, which has to do
with the notion of the pun. The parallel which Hartman draws
between *Glas* and *Finnegans Wake* is based, most of all, on
the importance of puns. This is something that both texts
share, Hartman maintains, and it is this that impels him to
suppose that 'There is a real danger of literature getting lost,
running amok or running scared after Joyce's *Wake* and
Derrida's *Glas* . . . Where the word was, the pun shall be' (79).
In keeping with this, then, Hartman describes *Glas* as 'a

scandalous literary pudding or French trifle' (63), endlessly 'punning' (see, for example, 15, 22) and 'punsterish' (46).

Against this, and against the readings of his work aligned with it, Derrida himself writes in the Foreword to the English translation of *Glas* (1986). This short text, entitled 'Proverb: "He that would pun ... " ', opens with the unequivocal assertion that *Glas* is not a punning text at all: 'Contrary to the rumor and to what some would like you to believe', Derrida declares, 'in that book [*Glas*] there is not one single *pun*' (Pro, 17). 'At least', he goes on to specify, there are no puns, there is no punning,

> if ... one persists in understanding by this word, as is so often done in certain socio-ideological situations and to defend certain norms, the free play, the complacent and slightly narcissistic relation to language, the exercise of virtuosity to no profit, without economy of sense or knowledge, without any necessity but that of enjoying one's mastery over one's language and the others. (18)

Under attack here, in particular, is the widespread misconception of Derrida's work as practising and promoting 'free play'. Again, Hartman's *Saving the Text* can certainly be seen as culpable in this respect: it repeatedly talks of 'free play' (see, for instance, 8, 22, 25, 62), despite the fact that this is not a term appropriate to or consonant with Derrida's work.

s

Yes, yes, and yet ... It may be remarked that Hartman's account of 'punning' in *Glas* is not perhaps as unequivocal as Derrida's own implied 'counterstatement' might suggest. Hartman's focus is not so much on what is 'complacent' or 'narcissistic', on what is self-indulgent or merely frivolous, but rather to the contrary on the sense that 'Every pun, in Derrida, is philosophically accountable' (22) and indeed that part of the problem with *Glas*, as opposed to the work of Joyce, is the fact that it is *not* humorous. Joyce 'shocks and delights', says Hartman, whereas Derrida 'teaches' (22). This is perhaps not the place to enter into a discussion of how side-splitting we find Derrida's *Glas* (with its text from the very start split in two sides), or of how far we might want to argue that teaching need not be opposed to shock and delight.[16] Let us instead try to elaborate a little further on the hypothesis that perhaps after all there is something in what Geoffrey Hartman says and that Derrida is responding to that something when he makes his declaration in the 1986 Foreword to the English translation of *Glas*.

t

Hartman questions Derrida on the signature as wound, observing that 'Derrida's "The signature is a wound and there is no other origin of the work of art" [*G*, 184] still links the wound to identity loss' (60). Hartman's argument here might be glossed as follows: contrary to the rumour and to what many might like to believe, Derrida is still holding on to the principle of identity underneath it all; he may claim that the human subject must be deconstructed but, look, he's still seeing the origin and production of the work of art in terms of identity. In this, I believe, Hartman is quite correct. To the extent that Derrida's 'Proverb' might be taken as a riposte to such formulations, however, I would argue that it is necessary (1) to take rigorous account of what he has to say, for example, about the notion of signature in relation to identity, and about the notion of the pun in relation to narcissism and 'mastery over one's language'; and (2) to try, in the wake of this, to elaborate an at least provisional sense of the work of Derrida and Hartman in terms that are not simply reducible or recuperable to an agonistics. I would suggest that if Hartman and Derrida have something to tell us, it has to do with evacuating the arena of such an agonistics: it has to do with multiple voices and with the very opening of the future.

u

What makes the signature a wound is not something that happens to a self-identical subject, a subject whose identity precedes either its signature or the wound it embodies. Derrida nowhere simply *denies* the principle of identity or 'the founding value of presence' (*SP*, 7). Rather he is concerned to show that the notions of signature, proper name, identity, singularity, etc. are made possible only by the logic of a contaminating generality. The proper name, for example, is haunted; it carries death. As Derrida puts it in a discussion in *The Ear of the Other*: 'every name is the name of someone dead, or of a living someone whom it can do without' (*EO*, 53). In this respect, we might say, every name is mortally marked or wounded. Every signature is divided; 'the signature is deviant, in and of itself' (*P*, 100, n.9). There is no signature without an engagement to a law of repeatability which compromises the identity and singularity of that signature. It is for this reason that Derrida can say, for example, that he doesn't believe 'that there is anything inimitable' (*EO*, 110). Derrida nowhere proposes a *junking* of identity, nor would he deny the effectivity of the notions of narcissism and 'mastery over one's language'. His concern is, however, to show how these notions are themselves always already dislocated, contaminated, haunted.

v

Starting, for example, with the voice, and with the experience of hearing oneself speak. *Saving the Text* concludes with the resounding, Lycidasical assertion that 'the "dread Voice" exists as the poem or not at all' (157). It is clearly the case that a sense of that 'dread voice' also empowers the logic, the multivocality and polytonality, of Derrida's work, not least for example in its emphasis on the sense of being 'Terrified by the difference within hearing-oneself-speak' (QQ, 291) or on the sense that every experience of voice is necessarily haunted by fiction, prosopopoeia and death.[17] Hartman's book, like so many of Derrida's texts, closes on the threshold, closing without closing, closing with the sense of a responsiveness to, a responsibility towards, a summons, a calling or invocation. The 'dread voice' is to come, just as — in Derrida — there is the call of the other to 'come', in an intolerable vibration of multiple voices.[18]

w

Derrida's proposition that 'the signature is a wound', for
example, glosses or glossolates a passage from Jean Genet
(cited in *G*, 184): in whose voice should it be heard? Marked
by laughter as well as by death, wouldn't this voice always
be double and more than double, in short is it not a kind of
pun? 'Voice' here might be figured as a pun in the sense
precisely that it is not so much homophonic as heterophonic:
it always lends itself to the play of becoming other and of
being heard otherwise. As Derrida suggests in 'Ulysses Gramophone', there is a 'yes' or rather a double 'yes' that precedes
every voice, and this strange 'pun' might be construed as the
condition alike of hilarity and dread. Just as voice cannot be
theorised simply in terms of polyphony, but evokes what
Derrida elsewhere refers to as 'a vocal *difference* rebellious to
any opposition' — a kind of vocality *in reserve*, which 'remains
neither at the service, organ or signifying power of a person
or of a self; nor of a conscious or unconscious; nor of any of
the two sexes' (v ii, 81) — so the notion of pun cannot be held
within a theory of polysemia or a play of several meanings but
always already opens on to dissemination. The very identity
of the word 'pun' is necessarily divided within itself, its very
possibility being dependent on a logic of iterability which by
the same token dislocates it.[19] Thus, no mastery when it
comes to the pun: as Derrida suggests elsewhere, 'Iterability
is at once the condition and the limit of mastery: it broaches
and breaches it' (LI, 107).

x

I would like to conclude by considering some of the foregoing
remarks in relation to Wordsworth's 'The Solitary Reaper':

> Behold her, single in the field,
> Yon solitary Highland Lass!
> Reaping and singing by herself;
> Stop here, or gently pass!
> Alone she cuts and binds the grain,
> And sings a melancholy strain;
> O listen! for the Vale profound

Is overflowing with the sound.

No Nightingale did ever chaunt
More welcome notes to weary bands
Of travellers in some shady haunt,
Among Arabian sands:
A voice so thrilling ne'er was heard
In spring-time from the Cuckoo-bird,
Breaking the silence of the seas
Among the farthest Hebrides.

Will no one tell me what she sings? —
Perhaps the plaintive numbers flow
For old, unhappy, far-off things,
And battles long ago:
Or is it some more humble lay,
Familiar matter of today?
Some natural sorrow, loss, or pain,
That has been, and may be again?

Whate'er the theme, the Maiden sang
As if her song could have no ending;
I saw her singing at her work,
And o'er the sickle bending; —
I listened, motionless and still;
And, as I mounted up the hill,
The music in my heart I bore,
Long after it was heard no more.[20]

How might we read this poem, after Hartman and after
Derrida? To try to read it, or listen to it, is no doubt to attune
oneself to the potentially affective 'power of music', to the
'thrilling', 'overflowing' effects of a voice, and to what Derrida
calls 'hidden possibilities in the language' (DTJ, 6). This little
poem is, I would argue, like nuclear waste. In 'Biodegradables'
Derrida writes:

> [A text] must be assimilated as inassimilable, kept in reserve,
> unforgettable because irreceivable, capable of inducing meaning
> without being exhausted by meaning, incomprehensibly ellipti-
> cal, secret. What is it in a 'great' work, let's say of Plato, Shake-
> speare, Hugo, Mallarmé, James, Joyce, Kafka, Heidegger,
> Benjamin, Blanchot, Celan, that resists erosion? What is it that,

far from being exhausted in amnesia, increases its reserve to
the very extent to which one draws from it, as if expenditure
augmented the capital? This very thing [*cela même*], this singular event that, enriching the meaning and accumulating memory,
is nevertheless not to be reduced to a totality or that always
exceeds interpretation. What resists immediate degradation is
this very thing, the text or in the text, which is no longer on the
order of meaning and which joins the universal wealth of
the 'message' to unintelligible singularity, finally unreadable (if
reading means to understand and to learn to know), of a trace
or a signature. The irreplaceable singularity, the event of signature, is not to be summed up in a patronymic name, because it
is the work itself. The 'proper name' in question — which has
no meaning and is not a concept — is not to be reduced to the
appellation of civil status. What is more, it is proper to nothing
and to no one, reappropriable by nothing and by no one, not
even by the presumed bearer. It is this singular impropriety that
permits it to resist degradation — not forever, but for a long
time. Enigmatic kinship between waste, for example nuclear
waste, and the 'masterpiece'. (Bio, 845)

One might say that 'The Solitary Reaper' provides a kind of
allegory of the 'singular impropriety' that Derrida speaks
of and that 'resists degradation'. In whose voice is this poem
to be heard or read? *Is* there a solitary reaper? What is this
music which cannot be identified ('Will no one tell me . . .?')
but which is apparently incorporated, encrypted, borne with
a strange continuing half-life, a half-life which in some sense
has been and continues to be transferred to future generations?

To read this poem, I would suggest, is to be drawn into
an experience of voice as irreducibly plural and ghostly. It is
to acknowledge that the poem *seems* in some respects highly
accessible, assimilable, 'open', and yet at the same time it
resists, it is elliptical, it exceeds interpretation. The logic of a
double-bind cuts and binds the title: how does one read it?
to whom is it addressed? to whom or to what does it finally
refer? does one (as reader) stop, or gently pass? or does one
pass *by* stopping or stop *by* passing? what is the stop-or-go,
stop-and-go, of a title?

Garrett Stewart has drawn attention to the ambiguity of
the opening line of the poem and the effects of hearing/reading

'Behold her' as 'Beholder'.[21] He notes that 'our identification
with the reaper (herself perhaps a beholder too) extends to
the figurative sense of reading as its own version of garnering
in solitude' and goes on to consider the 'deconstructive
linguistics' whereby 'That apostrophic gesture, "Behold her",
constitutes an address to an always, in one sense, absent
reader who, even when present to the words of the text,
beholds never more than the words'.[22] One might take this
phonemic reading further — for example towards a more
radical questioning of whether reading can ever be 'garnering
in solitude' and whether one can ever be only and simply
'present to the words of the text'. Present to which words
and in what present? Wordsworth's poem not only makes the
temporal locus of the subject of what is sung 'irreceivable' (is
the singing about 'long ago', about 'today', or about what
is still to come or what 'may be again'?) but also renders
'inassimilable' what might be called the time of its own narration and of its own reading.

   If the opening of the poem freezes the reader or beholder
in a (phantasmagoric) present — suspending her or him
before the stoniness of these words (as if, in Paul de Man's
phrase, transporting the reader 'into the frozen world of the
dead')[23] while marking the impossible synaesthetic demand
that s/he see sound ('Behold her[,] sing — ')[24] and perhaps,
at the same time, see or hear the eerily speaking 'single Field'
of what the 'I'/eye has 'looked upon' in the Intimations
Ode[25] — the final stanza of 'The Solitary Reaper' belongs to
another or other times. The beginning of this final stanza
shifts from the present ('what she sings') to the past
('Whate'er the theme, the Maiden sang . . .'), but this past is
cut and bound, split and divided in multiple ways, including
at least (1) the sense of a past that 'could [?] have no ending';
(2) the sense of the past in which 'I' 'saw'; (3) the sense of
the past in which 'I mounted up the hill'; and (4) the sense
of the past 'long after it [the singing, primarily] was heard no
more' — a past which, on one reading at least, would seem
indeed to 'have' or have had 'no ending'.

   In this final stanza, which in a sense leaves *us* standing
still, 'I saw her singing' seems to function as an uncanny
affirmation of the synaesthesia invoked (or, as Stewart might

say, 'evocalised') earlier. The ghostliness of the 'I' in the final
stanza is generated in part by this synaesthesia; in part by the
sense of *another* reaper, wavering in the deathly, syntactical
uncertainty (however fleeting) of who or what is 'bending'
'o'er the sickle'; and in part by the strangeness of 'still':

> I saw her singing at her work,
> And o'er the sickle bending; —
> I listened, motionless and still;
> And, as I mounted up the hill . . .

The word 'still' is not only polysemic — bearing a sense of
'silent', 'calm', 'quiet', as well as evoking — however paradoxi-
cally — the adverbal sense of 'always', 'up to the present
time'. 'Still' is at once disseminatory and cryptic: it figures
the still heart of this text, and even, I would suggest, the
entire oeuvre identified with the proper name and signature
of Wordsworth. It resists being read, it is *still* to be read. The
whole of Wordsworth's work is buried and borne in this word,
and yet — to pick up some of the 'hidden possibilities' in
the words of Derrida (Derrida whose work has not yet been
received, whose work precisely *resists* being received, keeping
itself in reserve, in spite of itself) — 'still' is 'proper to nothing
and to no one'. Anonymous or, better perhaps, pre-
anonymous.

                                    y

Breaking the silence of the seas.

                                    z

The hydrapoetic effects of hearing voices after Hartman and
Derrida, through 'The Solitary Reaper', engage what may be
called the radically amateur. 'Amateur' here involves not only
a sense of the lover and of that love which is a condition of
any deconstructive reading,[26] but also a deconstruction of the
'professional' as such. Might we not dream of a kind of critical
writing that would be a deconstruction of profession, of every
professionalism and professing? — not in the name of some
traditional, hierarchically opposed notion of amateurism (like

that of the amateur man or woman of letters, the 'mere' 'amateur'), but rather as part of an acknowledgement and elaboration of the fact that every professor or professional, and every profession worthy of its name, is radically amateur. Such a writing would try to take account of the perhaps finally abyssal irony of 'professing' — that professing always carries a force of irreducible duplicity, a sense of claiming or pretending[27] — and lead us towards a notion of professing and professionalism that would no longer be grounded in the assumption of a self-identical subject who professes. This kind of critical writing would, perhaps, no longer be literary criticism. To adopt a remark of Derrida's, in the context of a discussion of literature and literary criticism: 'we must invent [names] for those "critical" inventions which belong to literature while deforming its limits' (TSICL, 52). Hydrapoetics, a critico-glossolalia, a radically amateur writing: such designations imply a 'dream of passion' (in Hamlet's words) which precedes ego, subject or identity. Irreceivable. As simple as a, b, c.

Notes

1 Geoffrey H. Hartman, *Saving the Text: Literature / Derrida / Philosophy* (Baltimore: Johns Hopkins University Press, 1981).

2 For a thought-provoking recent essay on pre-anonymity, see Jeffrey A. Masten, 'Beaumont and/or Fletcher: Collaboration and the Interpretation of Renaissance Drama', *English Literary History*, 59:2 (1992), 337–56.

3 William Wordsworth, 'Ode: Intimations of Immortality from Recollections of Early Childhood', in *Poems, Volume I*, ed. John O. Hayden (Harmondsworth: Penguin, 1977), 526.

4 Yvor Winters, 'The Audible Reading of Poetry', *The Function of Criticism: Problems and Exercises*, 2nd ed. (Denver: Alan Swallow, 1957), 79–100; Garrett Stewart, *Reading Voices: Literature and the Phonotext* (Berkeley: University of California Press, 1990).

5 See Geoffrey H. Hartman, *Minor Prophecies: The Literary Essay in the Culture Wars* (Cambridge, Mass.: Harvard University Press, 1991), 207.

6 At stake here is no doubt something like the Girardian model of the agonistic scene described in the essay 'Hamlet's Dull Revenge'

(*Stanford Literature Review*, 1:2 (1984), 159–200) in terms of 'the mimetic nature of human conflict and the resulting tendency of the antagonists to behave more and more alike as they perceive more and more difference between each other' (176). As I will try to suggest, the notion of writing in reserve would have to be figured as in some sense *preceding* identity, prior to every and any experience of ambivalence and any possible alleged mastery of the pun.

7 Alongside these, there is the provoking double-edged assertion, cited earlier, that 'Derrida tells literary people only what they have always known and repressed' (23). Here, it seems, Derrida is implicitly presented as non-literary — elsewhere, however, Hartman admirably emphasises the extent to which Derrida's work effects the mutual contamination and displacement of the categories of 'literature' and 'philosophy', though he does not perhaps go so far as he might in exploring the strangeness of the phrase 'literary people'.

8 The phrase 'jargon of civility' is from Hartman: see *Minor Prophecies*, 207.

9 Samuel Weber, 'The Limits of Professionalism', *Institution and Interpretation* (Minneapolis: University of Minnesota Press, 1987), 18–32.

10 For example by Geoffrey Bennington, 'Deconstruction and the Philosophers (The Very Idea)', in his *Legislations: The Politics of Deconstruction* (London and New York: Verso, 1994), 18, 52–3, n.26.

11 See also, for example, *Saving the Text*, 14, 21, 46, 90, 111, 151.

12 Linked to this, and in ways that are more than symptomatic of Hartman's own particular 'take' on Derrida, 'deconstruction' is not distinguishable from 'deconstructionism': the crucial importance of such a distinction (*and* lack of distinction) is outlined by Derrida in the essay entitled 'Some Statements and Truisms about Neologisms, Newisms, Postisms, Parasitisms, and other Small Seismisms' (SST).

13 See also DA, 16.

14 As for instance when he writes: 'Let me suppose, then, that words are always armed and capable of wounding: either because, expecting so much of them, looking to them as potentially definitive or clarifying, we are hurt by their equivocal nature; or because the ear, as a *psychic* organ, is at least as vulnerable as the eye. What is unclear about the first hypothesis is why we should expect so much of words' (123). In passing here, we might note that this statement's explicit privileging of the auditory, of the ear as '*psychic*' organ', relies suggestively on two figurations of the visual — the verbs *to expect* (*ex, spectare*) and *to look*. Our 'expecting' and 'looking' are in any case presented here as being in some sense prelinguistic or extralinguistic.

15 It should be noted, perhaps, that it remains true to say that nowhere in *Saving the Text* is there a clear indication that Hartman has grasped the more radical aspects of Derrida's notion of 'writing' as that which precisely is *not* written, as that which *precedes* the putative 'origin' or 'birth' of writing as such. This is evident when he asserts, for example, that Derrida 'knows perfectly well that what evidence we have indicates that writing is an after-birth . . . The *Nachträglichkeit* of written language is an after-pregnancy comparable to that of interpretation: the transcription in other or apparently secondary terms of something already given' (*Saving the Text*, 8). A similar kind of argument would be appropriate in relation to what Hartman calls 'the physicality of words' (59) — a physicality which he appears to assume, but which Derrida is concerned rather to question. The most exhaustive exploration of what has elsewhere (and problematically) been termed the materiality of language is perhaps Derrida's meditation on the 'thing' in *Signsponge* (*S*).

16 In *Glas* we may read: 'You have to know how to die of laughter . . .' (*G*, 129). To comment on those words alone — out of context, decapitated, as they are here — would merit at least one monograph. A question among other things, no doubt, of experiencing the impossible. (I discuss laughter and some of the comic aspects of Derrida's work at various moments below, especially in Chapter 4.)

17 See, in particular, *Mémoires for Paul de Man*, in which he suggests, for example, that 'prosopopeia remains a fictive voice, although I believe that this voice already haunts any said real or present voice' (*M*, 26).

18 See, in particular, AT and PIO.

19 It is with this in mind that we might approach the question of 'literature' and 'the secret' which Derrida associates with 'the functional possibility of homonymy or of *mimesis*' (POO, 21). For another account of the pun in relation to Derrida's work, see John Llewelyn, 'Responsibility with Indecidability', in *Derrida: A Critical Reader*, ed. David Wood (Oxford and Cambridge, Mass.: Basil Blackwell, 1992), 73–4.

20 William Wordsworth, *The Poems, Volume 1*, 659–60.

21 See Garrett Stewart, *Reading Voices*, 155–6.

22 *Reading Voices*, 156.

23 See Paul de Man, 'Autobiography as De-Facement', in his *The Rhetoric of Romanticism* (New York: Columbia University Press, 1983), 78.

24 Or, which may in some sense of course come to the same thing, that we as readers 'behold her' and ourselves 'sing'.

25 I refer to that astonishing turn in stanza IV: ' — But there's a Tree,

of many, one, / A single Field which I have looked upon, / Both of
them speak of something that is gone': see *The Poems, Volume 1*,
525.

26 See *EO*, 87. I consider the links between deconstruction and love in
further detail in Chapter 6, below.

27 The figure of the professor in this sense may be compared with that
of the legislator: both are undecidably charlatan. For a fine
account of this undecidability, see Geoffrey Bennington, 'Mosaic
Fragment: if Derrida were an Egyptian . . .', in his *Legislations: The
Politics of Deconstruction*, 207–26.

4

The remains of psychoanalysis (i): telepathy

> The gift is always a strike of force, an irruption.
>
> WB, 199

In the interview with Derek Attridge published in *Acts of Literature* (1992), Derrida talks about his time at school, in the 1940s, and his bewilderment when 'beginning to discover this strange institution called literature' (TSICL, 36). He states:

> Bewilderment, then, faced with this institution or type of object which allows one to say everything. What is it? What 'remains' when desire has just inscribed something which 'remains' there, like an object at the disposal of others, one that can be repeated? What does 'remaining' mean? (TSICL, 36–7)

All of Derrida's work can be read as an attempt to respond to this question of 'remains' — especially, but not only, to the question of 'remains as a written thing' (TSICL, 37). This is evident from the consistent deployment of a number of terms across his oeuvre, including the trace, remainder (*restance*), remains (*reste*), cinders (*cendre*), ruins and ghosts.[1] While these terms remain singular and heterogeneous, to the extent that they arise in different contexts and pertain to different expositions, they all serve to highlight Derrida's more general argument that remains are never simple and indeed that the notion of remains calls to be thought in terms of what was never present. Thus the challenge of Derrida's work as a whole comprises the difficulty of thinking remains *other than on the basis of what was once present*. The trace, for example, is not the remains of something that was once present and might be rendered present once again: rather it is that which prevents any present, and any experience of presence, from being completely itself, from ever coinciding with itself. In the final analysis, then, remains are always and only the remains of remains, just as there are always and only traces of traces.

There is no trace-in-itself, no remains-in-themselves. 'Nothing beside remains', to recall the words of that revenant from an antique land in Shelley's 'Ozymandias'. But Derrida's work suggests that remains, like ruins, are not negative: the cryptic structure they (impossibly) figure is, for him, linked to the most affirmative, even the only affirmative kind of thinking, affirmation itself.

What, then, of the remains of psychoanalysis?

It is part of the affirmative character of Derrida's thought that nothing is apparently repudiated, written off, dismissed:[2] thus, in the Attridge interview, he stresses that he has 'no desire to abandon... the memory of literature and philosophy', even though he is concerned above all with 'the dream of another institution', with a kind of writing, for example, that would be 'neither philosophy nor literature' (TSICL, 73). A similar point can be made with regard to the relationship between his work and psychoanalysis. The imperative of keeping the memory of psychoanalysis is clearly expressed in a short text entitled 'Let Us Not Forget — Psychoanalysis'. Here Derrida's passionate, psychoanalytically-informed engagement with the notion of a new enlightenment is articulated in contradistinction to those aspects of contemporary intellectual and culturo-political life that evidently embody a desire precisely to forget psychoanalysis. Outside 'Circumfession' (*JD ii*) what follows has to be one of the longest sentences in Derrida's work and this is not even the complete version. I cite, commencing with an ellipsis:

> ... people are starting to behave as though it was nothing at all, as though nothing had happened, as though taking into account the event of psychoanalysis, a logic of the unconscious, of 'unconscious concepts', even, were no longer *de rigueur*, no longer even had a place in something like the history of reason: as if one could calmly continue the good old discourse of the Enlightenment, return to Kant, call us back to the ethical or juridical or political responsibility of the subject by restoring the authority of consciousness, of the ego, of the reflexive cogito, of an 'I think' without pain or paradox; as if, in this moment of philosophical restoration that is in the air — for what is on the agenda, the agenda's moral agenda, is a sort of shameful, botched restoration — as if it were a matter of flattening the

supposed demands of reason into a discourse that is purely
communicative, informational, smooth; as though, finally, it were
again legitimate to accuse of obscurity or irrationalism anyone
who complicates things a little by wondering about the reason
of reason, about the history of the principle of reason or about
the event — perhaps a traumatic one — constituted by something like psychoanalysis in reason's relation to itself. (LUNFP, 4)

Derrida has written numerous essays on the work of Freud,
Lacan, and Abraham and Torok, and everything he has said,
for example, about memory, desire, mourning, crypts and
ghosts, demands to be read within the context of psychoanalytic concepts and their possible translations and transform-
ations.

This chapter and the one that follows are focused on 'the
remains of psychoanalysis' in quite narrowly-defined terms.
In particular I wish to consider the role and significance of
two kinds of 'remains' or 'remainders' in Freud's thought. The
first is the question of telepathy, the second is the so-called
Bacon–Shakespeare controversy. These two concerns may
appear marginal to Freud's work and thus to the foundations
of psychoanalysis. I would like to suggest, however, that they
can be seen as quite central — or, at least, as irremediably
interfering with the borders, the relations between what is
proper and what is not proper, what belongs and does not
belong, what is the inside and outside of psychoanalysis,
giving us a quite different archaeology of psychoanalysis and
the promise of another kind of thinking and writing. These
'remains of psychoanalysis' — which would not constitute
presences, rather the opposite — perhaps have as much to
do with the future of psychoanalysis as with its ostensive
history.

The comic writings of Jacques Derrida

Jacques Derrida can be so funny. It's no wonder people refer
to his 'superb comic prose' and talk about him as 'a great
comic writer'.[3] Yet this aspect of Derrida's work *remains*, to
date at least, comparatively unexamined. It may seem slightly
surprising to want to approach 'the remains of psychoanalysis' from this perspective, but in what follows I shall

attempt to justify it and to move towards some sort of clarifi-
cation of an observation and a question (or double-question)
which Derrida articulates in the course of what is, along with
'Limited Inc' (LI), perhaps his most celebrated comic essay
to date, that is to say 'Ulysses Gramophone: Hear Say Yes in
Joyce' (1984). Here he writes: 'It remains perhaps to think of
laughter, as, precisely, a remains. What does laughter want to
say? What does laughter want? [*Qu'est-ce que ça veut dire, le
rire? Qu'est-ce que ça veut rire?*]' (UG, 291).

My main focus here is another Derrida text, entitled 'Telepathy', published in 1981.[4] As well as being weird and (I can
confirm from so-called personal experience) more than
usually untranslatable, 'Telepathy' is also one of Derrida's
funniest works. In this essay or experiment — comprising,
like *The Post Card*, fragments of postcards, intermittent envois
without a nominally identified addressee — he considers one
of the two 'remains of psychoanalysis', that theme which,
together with the Bacon–Shakespeare controversy, 'always
perplexed [Freud] to the point of distraction [*bringen mich
immer aus der Fassung*]'.[5] This is the occult or, more specifically, the question of telepathy. As Derrida's essay suggests,
telepathy is a topic, a concept or phenomenon, which is
closely bound up with psychoanalysis but with which psychoanalysis cannot come to terms. Freud wrote a number of
lectures and shorter papers on telepathy and occultism,
of which Derrida declares: 'Until recently I imagined, through
ignorance and forgetfulness, that "telepathic" anxiety was
contained in small pockets of Freud — in short, what he says
about it in two or three articles regarded as minor' (T, 14).[6]
Derrida's 'Telepathy' could be described as deconstructively
exemplary in the sense not just that it is focused on some
putatively 'minor' or marginal texts, on the 'small pockets' of
another writer, but also that it is in turn presented as a minor
or marginal work, in relation to its author's other, ostensibly
more central and substantial texts. One could say that this
work entitled 'Telepathy' was remaindered before it was even
published. At any rate, it is from the outset offered as a
remains or remainder, as Derrida testifies in a footnote: 'Such
a remainder [*restant*], I am no doubt publishing it in order to
come closer to what remains inexplicable for me even to this

day . . . [It] should have appeared, as fragments and in accordance with the plan [*dispositif*] adopted at that time, in "Envois"
(Section One of *La carte postale* [Paris: Flammarion, 1980])'
(T, 38–9, n.1). In spite or perhaps because of its fragmentary
character, however, 'Telepathy' makes persuasive and important claims about the place of telepathy in relation to psychoanalysis. Derrida shows how the question of telepathy
disturbs psychoanalytic theory at its very core. It is, he suggests, 'Difficult to imagine a theory of what they still call the
unconscious without a theory of telepathy. They can be neither confused nor dissociated' (14). What is implied by this
proposition that a theory of telepathy and a theory of the
unconscious 'can be neither confused nor dissociated' is a
logic of the crypt or parasite, a logic according to which
'telepathy' becomes a kind of foreign body within psychoanalysis.

Derrida traces the history of this foreign body within the
chronology of Freud's writings and within the development of
the psychoanalytic movement. Freud has a lifelong obsession
with the question of telepathy but it is only in 1926 that
he announces his 'conversion'. But even then it is not a
public matter, according to Freud, this 'sin' of believing in
telepathy. As he tells Ernest Jones, in a letter dated 7 March
1926: 'When anyone adduces my fall into sin, just answer him
calmly that conversion to telepathy is my private affair like
my Jewishness, my passion for smoking and many other
things, and that the theme of telepathy is in essence alien to
psychoanalysis'.[7] As Derrida points out, 'this letter is contra-
dictory from start to finish' (T, 35). Not only, for example, is
it impossible rigorously to separate the public from the private here, to distinguish between on the one hand what the
founder of psychoanalysis subjectively and privately believes
and, on the other, what he objectively and publicly proclaims
in his writings; but it is also the case that Freud did after all
write a number of essays on the topic and indeed that the
concept of telepathy is significantly invoked in numerous
other of his writings including, for example, 'The "Uncanny" '
(*PFL*, 12: 335–76), 'The Theme of the Three Caskets' (*PFL*, 12:
233–47) and *Totem and Taboo* (*PFL*, 13: 43–224). In other
words, Freud's claim that 'the theme of telepathy is in essence

alien to psychoanalysis' is both right and wrong at the same time: the theme of telepathy is like a foreign body. From Freud's point of view, says Derrida, it is a question 'of admitting a foreign body into one's head, into the ego of psychoanalysis. Me psychoanalysis, I have a foreign body in my head . . .' (T, 35).

It is integral to the strangeness and power of a foreign body, in this context, that it has to do with both assimilation and vomit. This is how Derrida's essay concludes: 'So psychoanalysis . . . resembles an adventure of modern rationality set on swallowing *and* simultaneously rejecting the foreign body named Telepathy, on assimilating it and vomiting it without being able to make up its mind to do one or the other' (38, tr. mod.). If, as Derrida suggests, psychoanalysis disturbs and even traumatises 'reason's relation to itself' (LUNFP, 4), this 'adventure of modern rationality' is in turn traumatologised or traumaturged. Freud's 'conversion' in this respect is neither 'a resolution nor a solution, it is still the speaking scar of the foreign body' (38). Freud pussyfoots or, as Derrida puts it, practises the hesitation-waltz (*la valse-hesitation*) (15) around the question of telepathy, but even after his 'conversion', for instance in the lecture 'Dreams and Occultism' (*PFL*, 2: 60–87), we continue to hear 'the speaking scar of the foreign body'. A strange kind of hearing, to be sure, since the lecture entitled 'Dreams and Occultism' is, as Derrida observes, not really a lecture at all but rather a 'fake lecture' (see T, 18): although written as a lecture ('Ladies and Gentlemen [*Meine Damen und Herren!*]', it begins), it was never given. Indeed it is part of the foreign body nature of this affair that none of Freud's various so-called lectures on telepathy was ever delivered: 'Psychoanalysis and Telepathy' (1921) and 'Dreams and Telepathy' (1922) were likewise 'fake lectures' (see T, 18).

What is so funny about Derrida's 'Telepathy' has to do, at least in part, with the ways in which it mimics and upsets the tone of Freud's 'fake lectures' and with the ways in which it unsettles, dislocates and transforms distinctions between a public and private discourse, between science and belief, between the frivolity of a postcard and the sobriety of a scientific paper, between — last but not least — 'Freud' and

'Derrida' themselves. Permit me to extract and cite, for example, as follows:

> What a strategy, don't you admire it? I neutralise all the risks in advance. Even if the existence of telepathy (about which I know nothing and about which you will know nothing, especially not whether I believe in it and whether I want to know anything about it), were attested with all its requirements, even if it were assured, *sichergestellt*, there would be no need to change anything in my theory of the dream and my dream would be safe. (T, 23)

Or, a bit later on: 'In my new fake lectures, I insist as always on reestablishing the legitimate order: only psychoanalysis can teach something about telepathic phenomena and not vice-versa' (29). In each case Derrida's text is making a perfectly serious point — that Freud is clearly resistant even to entertaining the idea that telepathy might fundamentally call into question some of the basic tenets of psychoanalysis (dreams as wish-fulfilments, the concepts of the ego, the unconscious, and so on) — but this perfectly serious insight is being offered in a very bizarre fashion. Insight, in effect, ceases to be out of sight. Derrida's text takes on the first person singular of Freud's voice and says what Freud may in some sense have thought — whether consciously or unconsciously (that distinction is precisely what is being dismantled here) — but never said.

Telepathy here would seem to be, at least from one perspective, an apocalypse or uncovering comparable to that dramatised in George Eliot's *The Lifted Veil*: Derrida's text is reading Freud's thoughts and, in a manner that also corresponds in remarkable ways with Eliot's work, these thoughts are intensely egocentric. Just as George Eliot presents her protagonist's 'participation in other people's consciousness' as an intolerable revelation of 'all the suppressed egoism . . . from which human words and deeds emerge like leaflets covering a fermenting heap',[8] so Derrida presents a markedly ego- centred rendition of what is going on in Freud's mind. Derrida's miming of Freud's thoughts as 'Totally autobiographical' (24), as relentlessly egotistical — preoccupied with personal ambition ('My theory of the dream', 23) and so-called private sexual fantasy (if only she could be 'my second wife' (see T, 30–1)) — is at once a kind of conservatism in Derrida and a source of fine comedy. Egoic discourse is conserved, at the same time as being ridiculed. To adumbrate a point I will be trying to develop further in various ways in the *remains* of the present study, I would like simply to remark that there is, by comparison, strikingly little sense in this Derridamime of the kind of post-egoic or 'psychotic raving' about which Leo Bersani has written in relation to the discourse of characters in the writings of Samuel Beckett.[9]

To get in touch with telepathy is 'to lose one's head, no more no less' (T, 20). But if this Derrida essay is about losing one's head it is also, and at the same time, about maintaining a balance. Derrida proceeds, as he puts it, 'like the trapeze artist I have always been' (7). Even more perhaps than the postcards of 'Envois' (E), 'Telepathy' suggests a deconstructive sense of confiding. If Freud's articles on telepathy are 'fake lectures because he confides in them so much, poor man' (T, 18), it would also be possible to characterise Derrida's own essay in this fashion — in particular to the extent that we may feel inclined to read it as fake postcards. In this respect every thought can seem undecidably fake, undecidably programmed: the conflations and fragmentations of identity in Derrida's text disturb the very *fides* of confiding and confidence.

Derrida writes as Freud. He writes *after* Freud no doubt, but he also inhabits, mimes, interpolates the prose, the tone and manner of Freud in ways that undermine confidence in general — the sense of Freud's confidence in himself and in his theories, the sense of Derrida's confidence as writer and of our own confidence as readers, the notion of confiding something to someone and especially of confiding something to oneself. What is meant by *confiding*? *Who* is confiding, in whom, and how? It is a distinctive feature of Derrida's work that it takes the text of another writer (Rousseau, Kant, Nietzsche, Ponge) in an unusually intimate embrace, citing, paraphrasing, rendering it in such a way that it is no longer straightforwardly possible to say that 'that is what the "earlier" writer is saying whereas Derrida on the other hand is saying this'. Such writing can itself be described in terms of a telepathic relation (is such and such a moment in 'Parergon', for example, a presentation of 'Kant's thought' or is it not rather some sort of transference and effacement of the singularity of 'thought' within or across texts?).[10] But this kind of critical telepathy finds its apogee in the essay 'Telepathy', for here Derrida goes beyond the grammatical, proprietorial boundaries of the 'I' which conventionally govern discourse, including his own. Freud is no longer 'he' but 'I' as well. If the strategies of Derrida's writing and reading are especially well-demonstrated in this essay, they are also *other* — no longer Derrida's, no more Derrida, bye now

Representations of telepathy

Up to this point it may appear that we have proceeded as if it were obvious what the word 'telepathy' means. There is a correspondence here, perhaps, with how Derrida writes about the term 'representation' in the essay entitled 'Sending: On Representation':

> If I read, if I hear on the radio that the diplomatic or parliamentary representatives (*la représentation diplomatique ou parliamentaire*) of some country have been received by the Chief of State, that representatives (*répresentants*) of striking workers or the parents of schoolchildren have gone to the Ministry in a delegation, if I read in the paper that this evening there will be a representation of some play, or that such and such a painting represents this or that, etc., I understand without the least equivocation and I do not put my head into my hands to take in what it means. (SOR, 319)

Comic prose on a comic pose, perhaps; but it is also the case that such conceptual breakthroughs as may be ascribed to Derrida's work pertain precisely to an unsettling of the accepted relationship between a given word and concept. As he asserts, without the least equivocation, in his thesis-defence, 'The Time of a Thesis: Punctuations': 'Every conceptual breakthrough amounts to transforming, that is to deforming, an accredited, authorised relationship between a word and a concept, between a trope and what one had every interest to consider to be an unshiftable primary sense, a proper, literal or current usage' (TTP, 40–1).

Derrida's 'Telepathy', along with other recent work done in this area, promotes nothing less than a deformation and transformation of what may once have been supposed to happen under the aegis of this word 'telepathy'. The linkage between psychoanalysis and telepathy is historically specific: as is well known, the rise of spiritualism and the emergence of modern psychology in the second half of the nineteenth century belong together. The word 'telepathy' was invented and first used by Frederic Myers in 1882; psychoanalysis came into being a few years later and it can be seen to have done so by marking itself off, not only in relation to other more or less medically and scientifically respectable forms of psychology, but also in relation to the occult.[11] In its original formulation, Myers tells his colleagues at the Society for Psychical Research in London, in December 1882: 'we venture to introduce the words *Telesthesia* and *Telepathy* to cover all cases of impression received at a distance without the normal operation of the recognised sense organs.' Freud's definition, which involves bringing together the concepts of telepathy and thought-transference (this is part of his 'pussy-footing': they can, he says, 'without much violence be regarded as the same thing' (*PFL*, 2: 69)) is very close to Myers's: telepathy and thought-transference, says Freud, concern the idea 'that mental processes in one person — ideas, emotional states, conative impulses — can be transferred to another person through empty space without employing the familiar methods of communication by means of words and signs' (69). We might underline, in these definitions, the importance of the *normal*, of what is *recognised* and of what is *familiar* ('the normal operation of the recognised sense organs', says Myers; 'the familiar methods of communication', says Freud).

It is also clear, however, that in historical terms the word 'telepathy' is part of an explosion of forms of communication and possibilities of representation. Telepathy (like 'telesthesia') is indissociably bound up with other forms of telemedia and teleculture whose emergence also belongs to the nineteenth century: telegraphy (*OED* first recorded usage: 1795), photography (1839), the telephone (1835), the phonograph (1877) and gramophone (1888), and so on. The emergence of the term 'telepathy' is moreover closely linked to the so-called decline of Christianity in European and North American culture: a belief in telepathy, in the late nineteenth century, often (though by no means always) appears to have provided a kind of substitute for a belief in God. Finally, it is possible to regard the emergence of the concept of telepathy as, in effect, epistemologically programmed within the Romantic concept of sympathy. Telepathy embodies both the hyperbolisation or extreme limit of sympathy and *at the same time* its opposite, that is to say a loosening or fragmenting, a dispersion and dissemination of the conceptual grounds of sympathy.[12] This dissemination is in part the challenge presented by Derrida's work on telepathy.

The effect of this work has been to shake up and transform the very criteria by which the 'normal' and 'familiar' are understood. As Claudette Sartiliot suggests, in an essay on 'Telepathy and Writing in Jacques Derrida's *Glas*', Derrida starts by drawing on what is, in some respects, the most 'familiar' because 'oldest' or most 'archaic' sense of 'telepathy' — that is to say, Derrida's essay goes back to the Greek *tele-pathein* which 'implies both the idea of distance (*tele*) and that of suffering, feeling, being touched (*pathein*) in its physical, emotional and aesthetic sense'.[13] What is distant feeling, feeling in the distance? What if all analysis, including psychoanalysis, is tele-analysis? How are thinking, pleasure, beauty, love *affected* at a distance, *as* distance? But Derrida's reading is not a nostalgic or quasi-Heideggerian etymologism (as Sartiliot's account might here suggest): it is not a question of getting home, of going back to some original meaning, the comforting womb or matrix of sense. As Derrida points out: 'The ultimate naivety would be to allow oneself to think that Telepathy guarantees a destination which "posts and telecommunications" fail to provide' (16). The interest of his account consists rather in the fact that, as Sartiliot puts it, 'telepathy breaches the discreteness and unity of the subject, as well as the systems of thought derived from it'.[14] Far from reinstating or retracing a purportedly original or proper meaning of 'telepathy', Derrida's essay opens up spaces of thought which dissolve all 'familiar' assurances of the sense of that word. In question, and under threat, here is what Derrida calls 'the truth': thus he speaks of 'the truth, what I always have difficulty getting used to: that non-telepathy may be possible' (13, tr. mod.).

'Outside the subject' (32). Derrida picks up this phrase and throws it off, in passing, as a definition of 'telepathy', a definition which Freud must at once appreciate and disavow: 'telepathy', says Derrida, 'that's what it is, the outside-the-subject, [Freud] knows the score' (32). Derrida's 'Telepathy' challenges us among other things to think telepathy (and indeed sympathy) no longer in terms of a relation between two or more subjects whose identity is already constituted and assured. Rather than conceiving telepathy as something supplementary, something added on to the experience of a subject, Derrida situates it in accordance with the logic of a foreign body, as being at once outside-the-subject and at the very heart of the subject.

Boiling water

Let us return to the remains of psychoanalysis, which is what we started out from. Let us briefly consider a passage that occurs at the end of one of the New Introductory Lectures, 'Dreams and Occultism' (1933). In this fake lecture Freud considers a number of accounts, anecdotes and experiences that have been related to him by his patients or which have concerned his own relationships with his patients. He weighs up the pros and cons of telepathy and thought-transference, and concludes as follows:

> If there is such a thing as telepathy as a real process, we may suspect that, in spite of its being so hard to demonstrate, it is quite a common phenomenon. It would tally with our expectations if we were able to point to it particularly in the mental life of children. Here we are reminded of the frequent anxiety felt by children over the idea that their parents know all their thoughts without having to be told them — an exact counterpart and perhaps the source of the belief of adults in the omniscience of God. A short time ago Dorothy Burlingham, a trustworthy witness, in a paper on child analysis and the mother [1932] published some observations which, if they can be confirmed,

would be bound to put an end to the remaining doubts on the reality of thought-transference. She made use of the situation, no longer a rare one, in which a mother and child are simultaneously in analysis, and reported some remarkable events such as the following. One day the mother spoke during her analytic session of a gold coin that had played a particular part in one of the scenes of her childhood. Immediately afterwards, after she had returned home, her little boy, about ten years old, came to her room and brought her a gold coin which he asked her to keep for him. She asked him in astonishment where he had got it from. He had been given it on his birthday; but his birthday had been several months earlier and there was no reason why the child should have remembered the gold coin precisely then. The mother reported the occurrence to the child's analyst and asked her to find out from the child the reason for his action. But the child's analysis threw no light on the matter; the action had forced its way that day into the child's life like a foreign body. A few weeks later the mother was sitting at her writing-desk to write down, as she had been told to do, an account of the experience, when in came the boy and asked for the gold coin back, as he wanted to take it with him to show in his analytic session. Once again the child's analysis could discover no explanation of his wish.

  And this brings us back to psychoanalysis, which was what we started out from. (*PFL*, 2: 86–7)

Nothing in this passage as a whole would suggest that Freud is sceptical about what is recounted, thanks to the 'trustworthy witness' Dorothy Burlingham. There are numerous fascinating details here: there is, for example, the paradoxical suggestion of the opening sentence (that telepathy may be, contrary to the evidence, 'quite a common phenomenon'); there is the even more surprising inversion by which we are asked to think again about the reason for children's belief in adult omniscience; and there is also the fact that telepathy is here figured in terms of a foreign body, and that the action of this foreign body is specifically described as resistant to psychoanalysis ('the child's analysis threw no light on the matter'). Linked to this is the curiously disjunctive one-sentence final paragraph: 'And this brings us back to psychoanalysis, which was what we started out from' (87). Derrida comments: 'Freud has such an awareness (or such a desire) of having himself thus arrived at the limit of psychoanalysis (inside or outside?) that he begins a new paragraph and in this way concludes the lecture (these are the last words and one doesn't know whether they mean that the return to Freudian psychoanalysis has just begun or remains to come: "Und damit wären wir zur Psychoanalyse zurückgekommen, von der wir ausgegangen sind": "And this brings us back to psychoanalysis, which was what we started out from". Started out from? Distant from?' (34) asks Derrida, without closing brackets.

Part of the force of Derrida's account of Freud's writings on telepathy is to highlight this sense of the limits of psychoanalysis and the (im)pertinence of what is 'off-the-subject'. Putting this slightly differently we could say that Derrida's text presents us with a rendering of Freud's work as *no longer psychoanalysis* or, more precisely, as *plus de psychanalyse*, both *no longer* psychoanalysis and *more than* psychoanalysis. A psychoanalysis *after* psychoanalysis, beyond psychoanalysis: the remains of psychoanalysis still to come. This exorbitance of psychoanalysis is in a sense *internal* to psychoanalysis, encrypted, traumatological. To say this does not amount to lending support to the conventional — if intractably complex — argument that certain 'later Freud' texts are not specifically 'psychoanalytical' but more a discursive mix of anthropology, sociology, etc. Rather it is to point to the specific strangeness of Freud's 'fake lectures' on telepathy and to pose the question: if these texts, these 'fake lectures' are no longer psychoanalytic discourse, *what are they?*

Derrida's essay initiates a response to this by suggesting that what these 'fake lectures' present us with is Freud no longer as psychoanalyst but *as writer.* This is demonstrated by the following passage from Derrida's essay, which is again a kind of thought-reading of Freud and in particular of the notion of Freud's work as hypnopoetic:

> Reality, when I talk about it, it is as if to send them to sleep, you will understand nothing of my rhetoric otherwise. I have never been able to give up hypnosis, I have merely transferred one inductive method onto another: one could say that I have become a writer and in writing, rhetoric, the production [*mise*

en scène] and composition of texts, I have reinvested all my hypnogogic powers and desires. (T, 25)

This writerliness might be illustrated, in relation to the passage from the end of 'Dreams and Occultism' cited earlier, by way of a little tele-parody. After Freud and after Derrida, then:

A short time ago, Dorothy Burlingham, a trustworthy witness, *eine vertrauenswürdige Frau* (but at the same time eine Frau who is a close friend of my daughter — 'close friend', what does that mean?[15] — Dorothy whose children were among Anna's first patients) — a trustworthy witness, then, who is also intimately tied up with the Freud famille, especially as regards the tele-psycho-scenario of parents and children, in a paper on child analysis and the mother (1932) published some observations which, if they can be confirmed, would be bound to put an end to the remaining doubts on the reality of thought-transference. Yes, bound to, bound to be bound, diable and double, now now, no psychotic raving here, let me see, let me see, ahem ahem, no one will ever know, no art to find the mind's construction in the face, as Edward de Vere put it, de Freud, deriver, tum-ti-tum, here I go again, all insane in our dreams, how can they possibly be ours then, never mind, not to worry, mind over matter, no matter, never matter, and another thing, while we're off the subject, what am I saying, who is this anyhow, stop writing, let me see, what does Dorothy Burlingham say exactly? She reported some remarkable events such as the following. Ahem: which 'event' or 'events' should I recount? Is it ever possible to recount an event, I ask myself, or do I? Yes, I mean no, not I, not this time, what time, does anyone have the time? Nor do I, what did I tell you? Wouldn't it make most sense, wouldn't it be most correct (*richtige*), to recount the example which the analyst herself considers to be 'the most striking'? Or perhaps she is not sufficiently trustworthy? I quote, to myself, if you know what I mean, you the massive but silent, phantasmagoric general public within myself:

> The most striking example that I know of a child being influenced by his mother's thoughts is the following: The mother was in analysis and in her hour she had a fantasy of throwing a jug of

boiling water over someone in a rage. She had witnessed a
similar scene in her childhood. An hour later she was sitting at
the table with her children. The younger child quarreled with
his older sister. He suddenly left the table and returned a few
seconds later carrying a glass of steaming water. He advanced
on his sister crying: 'You will see what I will do to you', and he
threatened her with the water. The action was entirely unusual
and unexpected from him. Where would such an occurrence fit
in the child's analysis? Had it really anything to do with the
child? If not, what is this strange form of communication?[16]

No, Dorothy, this may be your prize example but it cannot
be mine. There's something faintly absurd about that story,
unnecessarily violent as well. From a rhetorical perspective,
from the point of view of producing an ending to my fake
lecture that will leave things serene and under control and
yet, at the same time, beautifully suggestive and enigmatic as
regards the question of the value of everything I've been going
on about (going on about, I admit, without really knowing or
understanding what I have been going on about), it would be
much better to recount the earlier example which Burlingham
gives, the one about the gold coin. Now that would be the
perfect rhetorical paraph, exit or exergue — an 'event' which
seems to confirm the reality of thought-transference but
which at the same time allegorises the enigma of telepathy
by associating it both with the figure of a foreign body (but
what is a foreign body (*ein Fremdkörper*)? will I ever get round
to evaluating that particular puzzler? what is this '*Fremd*'-
effect?) and with the figure of value itself (a gold coin:
Goldstück). Yes, then leave it there, and claim that that brings
us back to psychoanalysis and that that is where we started
out from. Pretty topping rhetorical wheeze, what? Hallo?

Calling telepathy

If, as Jackie's account suggests then, Sigi's fake lectures
exceed psychoanalysis and present themselves as *writing*, as
the work of Freud not as psychoanalyst but 'as a writer', we
may still feel compelled to give a name to what *kind* of writing
we are dealing with here. And a simple answer to this would
be to say: telepathy, a new practice of writing and a new

theory of subjectivity. A title is always a promise (to borrow a formulation from *Mémoires* (*M*, 115)), and the title of Derrida's essay points the way. This text is neither psychoanalytical nor a text *on* psychoanalysis. But nor are Derrida's fragments 'simply' philosophical. To describe this kind of writing *as* telepathy is to argue for a rethinking of the telepathic and for the recognition of new kinds of writing the emergence of which is, perhaps, to be witnessed in various ways and in various places today.[17] In this context we could recall Maria Torok's haunting evocation, published in the Afterword to *The Wolf Man's Magic Word*:

> Telepathy could thus be seen as the precursor to a type of research that dares the imagination as regards oneself and others, that refuses to be imprisoned in systems, mythologies, and universal symbolic equivalents. Telepathy would be the name of an ongoing and groping research that — at the moment of its emergence and in the area of its relevance — had not yet grasped either the true scope of its own inquiry or the conceptual rigor necessary for its elaboration.[18]

The word 'telepathy' would function, then, as a paleonym — a new-old word which is not to be given up but rather to be maintained (precisely as one might maintain a cemetery), analysed and elaborated in terms of what has perhaps been 'buried or hidden or forgotten' in it.[19] Rather than think of telepathy in the ways in which Freud evidently wished or needed to, as a kind of adjunct, a private affair, a question or 'distraction' out at the very margins of psychoanalysis, the possibility now arises that telepathy might actually be seen as the reverse: the theory and institution of psychoanalysis might be reconfigured as being part of a still emerging concept of telepathy. Telepathy would be the remains of psychoanalysis.

At stake here is the contamination and dislocation of a philosophy or science constructed on the basis of a reduction or repression of play, especially in so far as this fabrication maintains itself as anthropocentric, subject-centred and identity-oriented (both in its politics and in its conceptual make-up). As Derrida notes, in a discussion in *The Ear of the Other*: 'One could demonstrate that every time a philosophy or

science claims to have constituted its own coherence in some
fashion, it has in fact been led to reduce the element of play
or to comprehend it by assigning it a place, to hem it in
somehow. Well, in this sense, Freud is a classical scholar or
philosopher' (*EO*, 68). Telepathy might then be seen as a
psycho-political engagement with a more radical figuration of
play. As Derrida goes on to suggest, in *The Ear of the Other*:
'In order to think of play in a radical way, perhaps one must
think beyond the activity of a subject manipulating objects
according to or against the rules, et cetera' (*EO*, 69). Telepathy — and its related paleonyms, telepsychology, telepatho-
logy, teletheory, tele-analysis ('there is only tele-analysis', says
Derrida (T, 9)) — would incorporate philosophy as well. If
telepathy is, as he puts it, 'the interruption of the psychoanalysis of psychoanalysis' (T, 37), it is perhaps equally the
interruption of the philosophical. Telepathy would be surprising, engaging a force of surprise, a call or summons, 'prior' to
philosophy. The very surprising of thought, telepathy would
present experiences of the impossible, in which the writer,
reader or thinker is uniquely interrupted through an impossible identification with the call of the entirely other. Like
deconstruction, telepathy is a response to a call and can
happen only in multiple voices.

Telepathy and literature

Irreducible to either psychoanalysis or philosophy, telepathy
would nevertheless keep the memory of psychoanalysis and
philosophy.[20] I would like to conclude by suggesting that,
while it exceeds conventional notions of the literary, telepathy
would also keep the memory of literature. Derrida's essay
ostensibly cuts itself off from the literary when it propounds
its epistolary hypothesis that 'one cannot say of the
addressee that s/he exists before the letter' (T, 6). This, says
Derrida, has nothing to do with, for example, identifying with
the hero or heroine of a novel. But while this is true (for the
surprise or interruption of telepathy would cut the lines of
any such naive identification),[21] we should not be blinded to
the fact that Derrida's essay is itself powerfully 'literary' —
and perhaps precisely to the extent that this is not explicitly

thematised. No doubt its literarity is of a sort that puts it along with those other twentieth-century 'nontraditional texts' which he talks about in 'This Strange Institution Called Literature' and which 'all have in common that they are inscribed in a *critical* experience of literature' (TSICL, 41). Derrida's 'Telepathy', that is to say, would exemplify a kind of metaliterary writing — its literarity dislocates and overflows 'this strange institution called literature'. What impels us to read Derrida's essay in terms of the literary is, above all, the manner in which its multiple voices (starting with 'Derrida' and 'Freud' but irreducible to these two) illustrate a theory of fiction as what Dorrit Cohn calls 'transparent minds'.[22] As I have argued elsewhere, it is difficult to imagine a theory of fiction, a theory of the novel, without a theory of telepathy.[23] The interdependence of the novelistic and telepathic is nowhere more clearly staged than in the fact that — at least in third-person narratives — characterisation has traditionally presupposed a telepathic narrator. Novels *are* telepathic structures. To speak of the telepathic rather than the omniscient here perhaps helps clarify the rapport between Derrida's 'Telepathy' and the theory and practice of the novel, especially in some of its recent manifestations and permutations.

It could be suggested, then, that Derrida's rhetorical strategy of reading and narrating Freud's mind participates in a more general contemporary breaching of the novelistic convention of the omniscient narrator. To take three, quite heterogeneous examples: Toni Morrison's *The Bluest Eye* (1970), Salman Rushdie's *Midnight's Children* (1981) and Dennis Cooper's *Frisk* (1991).[24] All of these novels can be called limit-texts in the sense that they disturb the criteria according to which they might be classified as novels, in particular in so far as they make the very principle of omniscient narration tremble and crack. This trembling and cracking is visible, for example, in the consequences of identifying the omniscient narrator of *The Bluest Eye* as Claudia. In the disruptive acknowledgement of the effective collapse of narration — how can Claudia be the omniscient narrator at the same time as being a partial narrator? — *The Bluest Eye* broaches another

kind of writing altogether. A similiar disturbance is at work in
Rushdie's text which — by exposing telepathy as the foundation of realist and magical realist fiction alike — points
towards a sense of what is 'more than telepathy', in other
words towards a reinscription of the telepathic as such. As
Saleem the narrator declares:

> My voices, far from being sacred, turned out to be as profane,
> and as multitudinous, as dust. Telepathy, then; the kind of thing
> you're always reading about in the sensational magazines. But I
> ask for patience — wait. Only wait. It was telepathy; but also
> more than telepathy. Don't write me off too easily.[25]

Finally Dennis Cooper's *Frisk* presents the reader with an
apparently omniscient narrator but then postulates the identity of this narrator in the first person, as a psychopath called
Dennis. It could be said indeed that the conceptual and even
affective power of Cooper's work rests not on its graphic
descriptions of fucking and murdering, or one should perhaps
say murdering and fucking little boys, for example, but rather
on the more Derridean *graphic* that accompanies it, that is to
say the ways in which what is *recounted* is inscribed within a
scene of writing that destroys the conventions of first and
third person narration as such. All three of these allegedly
'literary' texts perform, in their own singular and exemplary
fashion, a kind of deconstitution of the novel in so far as this
presumes a noncritical model of an omniscient narrator. In
this respect all three also demonstrate what Derrida refers to
as 'a *critical* experience of literature'. Read after or beside
Derrida's 'Telepathy', they spur the dream of completely different kinds of psycho-literary-philosophical writing.

Derrida observes, in the context of the word 'unconscious': 'I feel like laughing every time I write this word,
especially with a possessive mark' (T, 16). Derrida wants to
laugh, it seems, at least in part because this is writing: I feel
like laughing, he says, every time I *write* the word 'unconscious', and even more so when it is the unconscious *of* so-
and-so, 'my' unconscious, Derrida's unconscious, your unconscious. In its risky and eerie fashion, what I have been describing as 'telepathy' entails possible *jetties* for kinds of thinking
and research which depart from but do not return to a logic

of the ego or the unconscious. These telepathic jetties are articulated rather in relation to the affirmative force of another laughter, a laughter without a possessive mark, a laughter which belongs to no subject but rather to the affirmation of the other, which would be the affirmation of telepathy. So when the question is asked: 'What does laughter want to say? What does laughter want?', the answer without the least equivocation would be: Yes. This *yes* effaces 'all possible monologue' (UG, 299); it is a *yes* constitutive of the very possibility of 'psychoanalytic knowledge', 'a *yes* more ancient than knowledge' (296). 'Always in the form of an answer' (UG, 265): yes yes.

Notes

1 The complexities of engaging with the notion of remains in Derrida's work start of course with the question of translation, with what 'remains' in translation, or with translation *as* remains, etc. For three particularly obvious examples of texts pervasively concerned with remains, see *Glas* (*G*), 'Cartouches' (in *TP*, 183–247) and *Cinders* (*C*). Derrida makes some useful observations about the (un)translatability of *reste* and *restance* in *Limited Inc* (LI, 51–4).

2 See, for instance, his remarks in *The Ear of the Other*: 'I never repudiate anything, through either strength or weakness, I don't know which; but, whether it's my luck or my naiveté, I don't think I have ever repudiated anything' (*EO*, 141–2).

3 Derek Attridge, 'Introduction: Derrida and the Questioning of Literature', *Acts of Literature*, 12, n.16. Attridge here also alludes to an essay by Richard Rorty in which we are told: 'Apart from his incredible, almost Nabokovian, polylingual linguistic facility, [Derrida] is a great *comic* writer – perhaps the funniest writer on philosophical topics since Kierkegaard': see Richard Rorty, 'Two Meanings of "Logocentrism": A Reply to Norris', in *Redrawing the Lines: Analytic Philosophy, Deconstruction, and Literary Theory*, ed. Reed Way Dasenbrock (Minneapolis: University of Minnesota Press, 1989), 209.

4 Jacques Derrida, 'Télépathie', *Furor*, 2 (February 1981), 5–41.

5 See Ernest Jones, *Sigmund Freud: Life and Work*, vol. III (London: Hogarth Press, 1957), 419.

6 See Sigmund Freud, 'Psycho-Analysis and Telepathy', in *The Standard Edition of the Complete Psychological Works of Sigmund Freud*, trans. James Strachey (London: Hogarth Press), vol. XVIII (1955), 173–93;

'Dreams and Telepathy', in vol. XVIII, 195–220; 'Some Additional Notes on Dream Interpretation as a Whole', containing a section on 'The Occult Significance of Dreams', in vol. XIX (1961), 135–8; and 'Dreams and Occultism', in *New Introductory Lectures*, trans. James Strachey, in *PFL*, 2: 60–87. These various texts are also available in *Psychoanalysis and the Occult*, ed. George Devereux (New York: International Universities Press, 1970). References in the present chapter to the original German version of 'Dreams and Occultism' ('Traum und Okkultismus') are taken from Sigmund Freud, *Neue Folge der Vorlesungen zur Einführung in die Psychoanalyse* (Frankfurt: Fischer Verlag, 1992), 34–59.

7 Jones, III, 423–4; cited by Derrida (T, 35).

8 George Eliot, *The Lifted Veil* (London: Virago, 1985), 26, 19–20.

9 Leo Bersani, *The Culture of Redemption* (Cambridge, Mass.: Harvard University Press, 1990), 169.

10 For instance, in the section of 'Parergon' on 'The Colossal' (*TP*, 119–47), when Derrida writes, '. . . does not the distance required for the experience of the sublime open up perception to the space of narrative? Does not the divergence between apprehension and comprehension already appeal to a narrative voice? Does it not already call itself, with a narrative voice, the colossal?' (142): here we may indeed ask, 'Who is asking this and in what voice? And is the narrative voice that calls (itself) the colossal in "Kant", in "Derrida" or rather in both *and* neither?' But, then, who is asking *these* questions?

11 For two general accounts of the historical background here, see Henri F. Ellenberger, *The Discovery of the Unconscious: The History and Evolution of Dynamic Psychiatry* (New York: Basic Books, 1970), and Janet Oppenheim, *The Other World: Spiritualism and Psychical Research in England, 1850–1914* (Cambridge: Cambridge University Press, 1985).

12 It is in this context that we might consider the notion of telepathy as at once presence and death. 'Telepathy' offers, I think, a particularly clear sense of how Derrida writes. It is written as if off-the-top-of his head, if not exactly off-his-head. In its singular and rigorous fashion, it is undisciplined or, rather perhaps, adisciplinary. Contrary to those accounts which regard his work as opposed to the value of 'presence', Derrida's 'Telepathy' conveys a sense of brilliant spontaneity and espouses the value of immediacy in explicit terms: it is concerned with exploring 'the area of our immediate apprehension', 'pathies' and 'receptions' (13) and with the *idea* of telepathy as being 'an assurance finally' of 'complete presence' and 'fusional immediacy' (35–6). But, by precisely the same token, this is a matter

of death. As he elsewhere puts it: 'Plenitude is the end (the goal), but were it attained, it would be the end (death)' (ATED, 129). It might be said then, that telepathy in this sense would be death.

13 Claudette Sartiliot, 'Telepathy and Writing in Jacques Derrida's *Glas*', *Paragraph*, 12:3 (1989), 214–28: see 217.

14 Sartiliot, 215.

15 The phrase 'close friend' is used by Paul Roazen in his book *Freud and His Followers*, which Derrida cites in a footnote added to the proof-corrections (22 January 1981) of the first publication of 'Telepathy' in French (see T, 40, n.9).

16 Dorothy T. Burlingham, 'Child Analysis and the Mother (An Excerpt)', in *Psychoanalysis and the Occult*, 190–1.

17 To give only a few examples of recent representations and explorations of telepathy and teleculture more generally, see John Forrester, 'Psychoanalysis: Gossip, Telepathy and/or Science?', in his *The Seductions of Psychoanalysis: Freud, Lacan and Derrida* (Cambridge: Cambridge University Press, 1990), 243–59; Ned Lukacher, 'Introduction: Mourning Becomes Telepathy', in Jacques Derrida, *Cinders*, trans. Lukacher (Lincoln, Nebraska: Nebraska University Press, 1991), 1–18; Avital Ronell, *Dictations: On Haunted Writing* (Lincoln: Nebraska University Press, 1986) and *The Telephone Book: Technology, Schizophrenia, Electric Speech* (Lincoln: Nebraska University Press, 1989); and Gregory Ulmer, *Applied Grammatology: Post(e)-Pedagogy from Jacques Derrida to Joseph Beuys* (Baltimore: Johns Hopkins University Press, 1985) and *Teletheory: Grammatology in the Age of Video* (London: Routledge, 1989).

18 Maria Torok, 'Afterword: What is Occult in Occultism? Between Sigmund Freud and Sergei Pankeiev Wolf Man', in Nicolas Abraham and Maria Torok, *The Wolf Man's Magic Word: A Cryptonymy*, trans. Nicholas Rand (Minneapolis: University of Minnesota Press, 1986), 86.

19 See 'On Colleges and Philosophy' (OCP), especially 224.

20 Cf. TSICL, 73.

21 Cf. 'This Strange Institution Called Literature', in which Derrida confesses that 'deep down I have probably never drawn great enjoyment from fiction, from reading novels, for example, beyond the pleasures taken in analysing the play of writing, or else certain naive movements of identification' (TSICL, 39).

22 See Dorrit Cohn, *Transparent Minds: Narrative Modes for Presenting Consciousness in Fiction* (Princeton: Princeton University Press, 1978).

23 *Telepathy and Literature: Essays on the Reading Mind* (Oxford and

Cambridge, Mass.: Basil Blackwell, 1991), 17, 89 and passim.

24 Toni Morrison, *The Bluest Eye* (1970; London: Triad/Panther Books, 1981); Salman Rushdie, *Midnight's Children* (1981; London: Picador, 1982); and Dennis Cooper, *Frisk* (London: Serpent's Tail, 1991).

25 *Midnight's Children*, 168.

5

The remains of psychoanalysis (ii): Shakespeare

It is the ear of the other that signs.

EO, 51

I

To recall, very briefly, the point of departure for this two-part investigation of the remains of psychoanalysis: in his three-volume biography, Ernest Jones refers to a letter of 1922 in which Freud confessed 'that there were two themes that always perplexed him to distraction (*bringen mich immer aus der Fassung*)'. One was 'occultism' or 'the question of telepathy'; the other was 'the Bacon–Shakespeare controversy'.[1] What is the Bacon–Shakespeare controversy? Why did Freud (to borrow Derrida's words) lose his head on this subject? Who wrote Shakespeare?[2] Or what, *after Derrida*, might be the criteria for determining — and appropriate ways of describing, representing, indeed countersigning — the authorship of a particular text or number of texts? How does the so-called Bacon–Shakespeare controversy relate to the name of Freud and the institution of psychoanalysis? And how out of touch is all this with the question of telepathy?

The 'Bacon–Shakespeare controversy' is a misnomer. The question concerns whether or not William Shakespeare really wrote the plays, poems and sonnets attributed to him: Francis Bacon is only one of the candidates put forward as the 'real' author. There have been plenty of others, as Samuel Schoenbaum makes clear in the 100-page section of his *Shakespeare's Lives* (1970) entitled 'Deviations'.[3] Among them are Chapman, Raleigh, Jonson, the 6th Earl of Derby, the 5th Earl of Rutland, the Earl of Southampton, Edward Dyer, William Seymour, Patrick O'Toole of Ennis, Michel Agnolo Florio, his son John Florio, Anne Whateley, Edward de Vere, Christopher Marlowe ('the most recent to achieve wide notoriety' (621), says Schoenbaum), James I, Fulke Greville, Sir Thomas North,

Queen Elizabeth, and even 'occult forces' (573). . . . Some anti-Shakespeareana or 'anti-Stratfordian' discourse argues for collaborative authorship: such theories are designated 'groupist' and would include Harold Johnson's *Did the Jesuits Write Shakespeare?* (1910), H. T. S. Forrest's *The Five Authors of 'Shakespeare's Sonnets'* (1923), and Gilbert Slater's *Seven Shakespeares* (1931).[4]

The identity of the author as Shakespeare was not questioned until nearly a hundred and fifty years after his death. Only in the second half of the nineteenth century did the 'controversy' emerge as such. Delia Bacon's 'William Shakespeare and His Plays; an Inquiry Concerning Them' was published in *Putnam's Monthly Magazine* in 1856; William Henry Smith's privately circulated letter to Lord Ellesmere, entitled *Was Lord Bacon the Author of Shakespeare's Plays?*, came a few months later. Expansion was rapid. Schoenbaum writes: 'By 1884 the authorship controversy had stirred France, Germany, and India, as well as England and the United States, and it had produced over 250 books, pamphlets, and articles' (554). At this stage Bacon was the principal competitor and his position was bolstered in the 1880s when Baconians, stimulated by the fact that their master knew and wrote about ciphers, started producing 'cryptographic', 'cryptanalytical' theories. As Schoenbaum observes, 'The endeavor to strengthen the Baconian case took ever more extravagant forms' (583); but increasingly, too, other competitors were being put forward. The quantity and quality of published material in fact becomes quite overwhelming. Finally even the scholarly Schoenbaum seems in danger of losing his head.[5]

And what of Freud? A letter to Martha Bernays in 1883 suggests an early inclination towards a groupist (rather than specifically Baconian) position: '. . . it seems to me that there is more need to share Shakespeare's achievement among several rivals than to burden another important man with it' (cited by Jones, III, 459). Any later leanings towards Baconianism were finally to be wiped out by a book called *Shakespeare Identified as Edward de Vere, Earl of Oxford* (1920), written (as Ernest Jones pleasurably informs us) by 'an author with the unfortunate name of Looney' (III, 460). Freud read Looney's book twice (in 1926 and 1927) and became, says Jones, 'practically convinced of his conclusions' (III, 460).

Why did the so-called Bacon–Shakespeare controversy arise? Why were Freud and so many others obsessed, distracted by it? Samuel Schoenbaum suggests that 'it is perhaps a mistake to pursue a rational explanation' (554). But in his very next sentence declares: 'Yet one can understand the emergence of an anti-Stratfordian movement out of mid-century unease over the Shakespeare of the popular understanding.' This at least gestures towards the broadly but clearly political dimension: Shakespeare the poacher, or ex-butcher, whose parents were illiterate, etc., couldn't possibly have been the bard; only an aristocrat could. And later Schoenbaum will offer a further explanation, one that is in keeping with his prevailing emphasis on the lack of 'academic credentials' (615) among most anti-Stratfordians. Books like Looney's are appealing because, in them, 'Sober literary history is metamorphosed into a game of detection. . . . To such a game the cultivated amateur can give his leisure hours in hopes of toppling the supreme literary idol and confounding the professionals' (602–3).

But most of all, and most provocatively perhaps, Schoenbaum makes use of psychoanalytic concepts in order to explain the controversy: the concepts of identification and ambivalence, family romance and rescue fantasy, for example. In dealing with the case of Freud, in particular, the use of psychoanalytic theory becomes decisive, and Schoenbaum here relies quite heavily on an article by Harry Trosman, 'Freud and the Controversy over Shakespearean Authorship', published in 1965.[6] Trosman glosses that familiar but strange affiliation between psychoanalytic discourse and detective fiction: 'Looney's book must have made an immediate appeal to Freud because to a large extent Looney's method resembled his own' (493). He also employs the concepts of family romance and rescue fantasy. Schoenbaum follows, and picks up as well Ernest Jones's noting a similarity between Freud's attitude to the author 'Shakespeare' and the argument in 'Moses and Monotheism' that Moses was an Egyptian. Schoenbaum writes: 'Such obsessions reflect the operation of the Family Romance fantasy. The child, reacting against disap-

pointment with the imperfections of his parents, compensates
by replacing them with others of higher birth; he must be a
stepchild or adopted. In later life such fantasies of parental
idealization are transposed to a Moses — or [Earl of] Oxford'
(612).

And what of Looney? Schoenbaum reiterates Trosman's
account of the bizarre scene in which Looney attempts to
deposit with the Librarian of the British Museum a sealed
envelope containing written testimony to his 'priority of discovery' vis-à-vis the Earl of Oxford's authorship.[7] In doing
this, Trosman argues,

> Looney could well imagine that eventually his identity would be
> revealed as the original instigator of the Oxfordian position. In
> the same way that [Looney] states credit must be given 'to the
> great Englishman' who actually authored the plays, credit would
> then be given to him who had actually made the Oxfordian
> discovery first. (465)

And Schoenbaum adds: 'Looney's deliverance of his idol from
depreciation and obscurity exemplifies the rescue fantasy,
interpreted by Freud as the son's defiant wish to settle his
account with his father for the gift of life' (613).

Finally, then, there is the concept of ambivalence. Here
Schoenbaum refers to the manifestations of 'filial ambivalence
throughout the dreary pages of anti-Stratfordian discourse: on
the one hand, denigration of the drunken, illiterate, usurious
poacher from the provinces; on the other, ecstatic veneration
of the substitute claimant, aristocrat and deity' (612). This
kind of manifestation of ambivalence is obvious enough in
Looney's *Shakespeare Identified* — the book Freud re-read,
says Schoenbaum, 'with no accessions of doubt' (609). What
goes for Looney, goes for Freud.

Ambivalence is clearly in play in Freud's own remarks, in
his 'Address Delivered in the Goethe House at Frankfort'
in 1930, on the value of biographies of great writers such as
Goethe and Shakespeare:

> But what can these biographies achieve for us? Even the best
> and fullest of them could not answer the two questions which
> alone seem worth knowing about. It would not throw any light
> on the riddle of the miraculous gift that makes an artist, and it

could not help us to comprehend any better the value and effect of his works. And yet there is no doubt that such a biography does satisfy a powerful need in us. We feel this very distinctly if the legacy of history unkindly refuses the satisfaction of this need — for example in the case of Shakespeare. It is undeniably painful to all of us that even now we do not know who was the author of the comedies, tragedies and sonnets of Shakespeare; whether it was in fact the untutored son of the provincial citizen of Stratford, who attained a modest position as an actor in London, or whether it was, rather, the nobly-born and highly cultivated, passionately wayward, to some extent *déclassé* aristocrat, Edward de Vere, seventeenth Earl of Oxford, hereditary Lord Great Chamberlain of England. (*PFL*,14: 470–1)

Freud goes on to argue that the 'powerful need' which biography can satisfy consists in bringing us closer to the artist 'as a human being'. This in turn involves the concept of ambivalence. A movement, then, towards 'degradation', since 'our reverence . . . regularly conceals a component of hostile rebellion' (471–2). Freud's own ambivalence towards the author of the comedies, tragedies and sonnets is thus explicit: ambivalence is 'a psychological fatality', he says; 'it cannot be altered without forcible suppression of the truth and is bound to extend to our relations with the great men whose life histories we wish to investigate' (472). But in the case of Shakespeare — in the absence of the greatly desired 'biography' or 'life history' — Freud's ambivalence is forced to operate at the level of the proper name of the author: what more magnificent degradation, one might ask, than to deny Shakespeare authorship of 'his' oeuvre?

But at this point we must pause. Briefly we have seen how Schoenbaum, following Trosman, seeks to use psychoanalytic theory to 'explain the unconscious origins of anti-Stratfordian polemics' (613). This entails a troubling paradox: namely, that both writers employ psychoanalytic theory in order to explain what Schoenbaum calls a 'surprising and sad' (608) aberration on the part of the founder of psychoanalytic theory. In *The Post Card*, Derrida demonstrates, through a reading of *Beyond the Pleasure Principle* (1920), how the institution of psychoanalysis is inextricably tied up with the name of its founder.[8]

There are threads here leading into the 'Bacon–Shakespeare controversy': I propose to analyse them.

Freud's own suspicions about the name of the first Baconian in print — Delia Bacon — clarify the stakes. Any inclination towards a strictly Baconian position was much diminished when (as Jones puts it) Freud 'heard that one of the founders of the Baconian idea was a Miss Bacon, of Boston, which suggested a personal reason for the cult' (III, 459–60). It is a question of the proper name. Freud's losing his head, being driven to the point of distraction over the 'Bacon–Shakespeare controversy', cannot be reduced simply to notions of family romance or rescue fantasy, whatever their exemplary status or value. Freud's engagement is, besides anything else, an engagement with the power of the proper name, his own and Shakespeare's. It is a question of the interrelations of proper name, institution and monumentalisation.[9] Of, among other things, 'psychoanalysis' and what we can provisionally call 'literature'.

Schoenbaum's 'Deviations' confirms the conclusions reached by the Friedmans some years earlier.[10] Anti-Stratfordian writings are exposed for all their 'intrinsic worthlessness' and 'ignorance of fact and method' (627–8); there are no grounds for believing a Baconian or indeed *any* other-author theory; Freud was wrong; in the absence of firm 'evidence' to the contrary, we should continue to suppose that the author of the plays and sonnets was William Shakespeare.

And yet, despite a systematic rubbishing of anti-Stratfordian positions, doubts may recur. As the Friedmans conclude their study of 1957: 'As to the main issue — we are left where we were: unable to state positively who wrote the plays.'[11] Samuel Schoenbaum's own interest in the complexities of this topic is reflected in his earlier study, *Internal Evidence and Elizabethan Dramatic Authorship*, published in 1966. He includes, among his final remarks, the following:

> We want to know; something there is that doesn't love an anonymous play. And so scholars use internal evidence as a basis for attribution. Some of the hypotheses are much better supported than others; some are almost certainly correct. But all of them remain hypotheses. Despite the safeguards devised, a subjective element resides in all attribution work, and even the utilization

of electronic computers will not eliminate the need for the exercise of scholarly judgment.[12]

What's in a name? Who wrote Shakespeare? How useful are the established notions of internal and external evidence in formulating a solution to this question?

Let us now turn to a more recent theorisation of these problems — to a text which pursues this questioning, works over the limits of 'scholarly judgment', disrupts distinctions between 'internal' and 'external evidence', and opens up new ways of thinking about authorship in general.

II

Derrida's *Signsponge* has been described as 'the most irruptive essay on literature' to have appeared in English this century.[13] It is also one of his most difficult texts, as well as one of his most daring. Explicitly and provocatively 'taking chances', the essay necessarily articulates itself in the uncanny and perhaps finally undecidable space between science and belief.[14] As regards the question of literary criticism, it would appear to represent a particularly strange and intense challenge. For nothing in the thought of *Signsponge* would justify critical recuperation within the traditional realms of so-called rationality or commonsense. *Signsponge* is simply irreducible to them. The essay effectively summarises the unprecedented range of its concerns:

> The critic and the philologist (and various others)... may wonder whether a certain piece of writing is indeed assignable to a certain author, but as regards the event of the signature, the abyssal machinery of this operation, the commerce between the said author and his proper name, in other words, whether he signs when he signs, whether his proper name is truly his name and truly proper, before or after the signature, and how all this is affected by the logic of the unconscious, the structure of the language, the paradoxes of name and reference, of nomination and description, the links between common and proper names, names of things and personal names, the proper and the non-proper, no question is ever posed by any of the regional disciplines which are, as such, concerned with texts known as literary. (*S*, 24, 26)

Derrida's *Signsponge* works on the work of Francis Ponge,
works on his name. It is concerned with notions of proper
name and signature.

Why write? What can writing do? A writer 'expresses his
name, and that is all. Across the entire corpus' (S, 70). Richard
Rand has elaborated: 'The drive is to take the proper name,
one's own name, and convert it into the signature, a mark
that will never perish. One can go so far as to say that the
artist doesn't give a damn about his work, he cares only about
the survival of his signature.'[15]

But if there is always some signature and always signature-
effects, it is also true that the signature never entirely
coincides with itself, it never takes place as an absolutely
proper and pure event. As Derrida makes clear in 'Signature
Event Context': 'In order to function, that is, to be readable,
a signature must have a repeatable, iterable, imitable form; it
must be able to be detached from the present and singular
intention of its production. It is its sameness which, by cor-
rupting its identity and its singularity, divides the seal [*sceau*]'
(SEC, 20). This strange logic of sameness and singularity, of
repetition and alterity, operates as the condition of possibility
of the signature. 'The necessarily invisible quotation marks
surrounding the proper name' (*S*, 8) must be acknowledged.
The signature can never be purely and simply present, proper,
self-identical, singular; it always involves, as well, (non-
simple) absence, the improper or non-proper, and otherness.
The notion of otherness is introduced, for example, as soon
as one raises questions about 'the line between the autography of one's proper name and a signature' (*S*, 54). As Derrida
does in *Spurs*: 'What, after all, is handwriting? Is one obliged,
merely because something is written in one's hand, to assume,
or thus to sign it? Does one assume even one's own signature?'
(*Sp*, 127).

Otherness is linked to the notion of 'the thing'. The drive
is to leave one's mark in the text itself; but 'by not letting the
signature fall outside the text anymore, as an undersigned
subscription, and by inserting it into the body of the text, you
monumentalize, institute, and erect it into a thing or a stony
object. But in doing so, you also lose the identity, the title of
ownership over the text: you let it become a moment or a

part of the text, as a thing or a common noun' (*S*, 56). Always the strange and paradoxical logic — that 'the stony monumentalization of the name (is) a way of losing the name' (26); that 'The signature is the placement in abyss (of the proper) itself: exappropriation' (132). There is always this 'double band' of the signature — 'stretched between the need to become a thing, the common name of a thing, or the name of a generality losing the *idion* in order to inscribe the colossal, and, on the other hand, the contrary demand for a pure idiomaticity, a capital letter unsoiled by the common, the condition of the signature in the proper sense' (64). There may be 'the momentary singularity of a certain coitus of signatures' (50) and this may consist in a certain union of signature ('pure idiomaticity') and countersignature (that of 'a thing' or 'a generality'). It may consist in 'the rebus signature, the metonymic or anagrammatic signature'; but 'these are the condition of possibility and impossibility. The double bind of a signature event' (64).

The only desire is to leave one's mark, to monumentalise one's name. The entire problematic comes forcefully in that single sentence from *Glas* which we cited Geoffrey Hartman citing earlier: 'The signature is a wound, and there is no other origin for the work of art' (*G*, 184). So what's in the name of 'Shakespeare'? How would *Signsponge* work in relation to the texts of 'Shakespeare'?

III

Freud's reading of *Hamlet*, in *The Interpretation of Dreams* (1900) (*PFL*, 4), illustrates with an almost embarrassing clarity the dangers of literary psychobiography. To take *Hamlet* as a real person, who has a 'mind' or 'unconscious' which can be probed and analysed; to declare that Hamlet's 'distaste for sexuality' would be shared 'more and more' by Shakespeare himself. . . . Freud also writes that

> *Hamlet* was written immediately after the death of Shakespeare's father (in 1601), that is, under the immediate impact of his bereavement and, as we may well assume, while his childhood feelings about his father had been freshly revived. It is known,

too, that Shakespeare's own son who died at an early age bore the name of 'Hamnet', which is identical with 'Hamlet'. (*PFL*, 4: 367–8)

It is now generally supposed that John Shakespeare's death did not antedate the composition of *Hamlet*; but it is known that Shakespeare's only son, Hamnet — 'of which name Hamlet is a variant form' (*Riverside*, 1828) — was buried at Stratford on 11 August 1596, aged eleven. Again, what interests us here is the name; and the fact that Freud, if only in passing, draws attention to it.

Freud's observations on the psychogenesis of *Hamlet* are rendered absurd by his own simple but amazing footnote, added in 1930: 'Incidentally, I have in the meantime ceased to believe that the author of Shakespeare's works was the man from Stratford' (368, n.1). But let us here cite Joyce's *Ulysses* (1922) which, interloping and interlooping between 1900 and the 1930 footnote, might be read as carrying on the analysis. As Stephen Dedalus says of the Ghost: 'To a son he speaks, the son of his soul, the prince, young Hamlet and to the son of his body, Hamnet Shakespeare, who has died in Stratford that his namesake may live for ever.'[16] In humour and in rigour *Ulysses* goes beyond Freud's account and, like the *Portrait* before it, explores the entire domain of the signature and proper name. Stephen says:

> He has hidden his own name, a fair name, William, in the plays, a super here, a clown there, as a painter of old Italy set his face in a dark corner of his canvas. He has revealed it in the sonnets where there is Will in overplus. Like John O'Gaunt his name is dear to him, as dear as the coat of arms he toadied for, on a bendsable, a spear or steeled argent, honorificabilitudinitatibus, dearer than his glory of greatest shakescene in the country. What's in a name?[17]

Allusions to the 'fair name' in *As You Like It* (V.i.22) and the Sonnets (for example, 57, 135, 136, 143), to the coat of arms granted to John Shakespeare in 1596, to one of the Baconians' favourite cryptonyms ('honorificabilitudinitatibus', in *Love's Labour's Lost*, V.i.41) and to Robert Greene's 1592 attack on the playwright as 'the onely Shake-scene in a countrey' (see

Riverside, 1835) — all of these culminate in the quotation from *Romeo and Juliet*: 'What's in a name?' (II.ii.43).

The idea of Shakespeare's authorship of Psalm 46, on the basis of the 46th word in, and the word 46 off the end; punning references to the name 'Will' in the sonnets; the sonnets' preoccupation with the name (for instance, 71, 72, 76, 95, 111) and, more specifically, with poetry as monumentalisation (for instance, 18, 19, 55, 63, 65, 74, 81, 107) — these are perhaps well-known. There are also contemporaneous descriptions of Shakespeare which link the ideas of name and monument — early meldings in the composition of the cultural Shakespeare-English-Monument (S.E.M.) text, the explosion of which may be witnessed not only in the recent work of new historicism or cultural materialism but, more disruptively, in reverber-ations at the very foundation of the monument, like that bang at the origin of the universe which Derrida speaks of in 'Tel-epathy', a noise which perhaps has not yet reached us.[18] One could unearth, for example, Leonard Digges's 'To the Memorie of the deceased Authour Maister W. Shakespeare' (*Riverside*, 71), which appeared in the First Folio:

> SHake-speare, at length thy pious fellowes giue
> The world thy Workes: thy Workes, by which, out-liue
> Thy Tombe, thy name must when that stone is rent,
> And Time dissolues thy Stratford Moniment,
> Here we aliue shall view thee still. . . .

Blurred syntax brings 'name' and 'Tombe' together. In Milton's 'Epitaph on the admirable Dramaticke Poet' (1630) (in *River-side*, 1845), the name requires no physical monument:

> What neede my *Shakespeare* for his honour'd bones,
> The labour of an Age, in piled stones
> Or that his hallow'd Reliques should be hid
> Vnder a starre-ypointing Pyramid?
> Deare Sonne of Memory, great Heire of *Fame*,
> What needst thou such dull witnesse of thy Name?
> Thou in our wonder and astonishment
> Hast built thy selfe a lasting Monument.

The name is itself a monument. It has been monumentalised into some other 'stony thing'. And there is an athanasy of the name — so long as appropriation, quasi-hypnotic identification, a singular kind of transference, translation no doubt, maintain 'William Shakespeare' as the thing ('my *Shakespeare*', a monument of 'wonder and astonishment', enough to 'make us Marble' as line 14 of Milton's poem has it).

IV

What's in a name? I wish to advance the following four hypotheses: (1) that *Signsponge* — and Derrida's other writings on the signature and proper name — appear to offer a way of identifying Shakespeare as author, a way which at the same time, however, tampers with traditional distinctions between 'internal' and 'external evidence', questioning the very idea of signing and appropriation (by the author, by the reader, in the name of the author, and so on); (2) that *Hamlet* can be read, then, not only as a text apparently signed, on the 'inside', by Shakespeare, but also (and *as if* in contradiction to this) as a text specifically concerned with the impossibility of signing; (3) that the logic of this reading can be extended to other 'Shakespeare' texts; and (4) that, finally, all of this can be linked up with the question of the remains of psychoanalysis and the proper name of 'Freud'.

Engaging disruptions between internal and external, Derrida argues that 'In the form of the whole name, the inscription of the signature plays strangely with the frame, with the border of the text, sometimes inside, sometimes outside' (*S*, 120). And again: 'a small part of the text, (the) *signature*, takes hold of the text, which it covers to the point that it also makes the text into a small part of itself, and therefore overflows it' (122). William Shakespeare expresses his name, and that is all, across the entire corpus. 'That every word doth almost tell my name' (sonnet 76): this proposition might be taken to illustrate what Derrida calls the second 'modality of signature', namely a 'set of idiomatic marks' which have 'no essential link with the form of the proper name' (*S*, 54).[19] But it also points us in the direction of the impossibility of the signature — in other words, towards a recognition of the *negative* force of this 'almost', the necessarily *residual* undecidability of every signature-event.

Derrida notes that 'The proper name, in its aleatoriness,

should have no meaning and should spend itself in immediate reference. But the chance or the misery of its arbitrary character (always other in each case) is that its inscription in language always affects it with a potential for meaning, and for no longer being proper once it has a meaning' (*S*, 118). He shows how this functions in and around the name 'Francis Ponge' — most elaborately in terms of the notion of 'sponge' (*éponge*; hence *signe-éponge, signé-ponge*). A similar situation clearly presents itself with Shakespeare. Again, it is perhaps worth stressing that this is not a matter of 'authorial intention', nor even of 'consciousness' or 'unconsciousness'. As Derrida points out in a discussion in *The Ear of the Other*: 'obviously this is not something one can decide: one doesn't disseminate or play with one's name. The very structure of the proper name sets this process in motion' (*EO*, 76). It may also be noted that the aim here is not simply to track down appearances of the proper name (however fragmented, displaced, homo- or heterophonic, anagrammatic, etc.) of an author, as if this could offer some kind of final reading or essential meaning; rather it is to explore the ways in which the writings identified with 'Shakespeare' can be seen to stage a deconstructive drama of idiom, proper name and signature in general.[20]

At the most obvious, commonsensical level then — before the others or not — the name has the at least doubly categorematical signification hinted at by Leonard Digges's hyphenation 'SHake-speare': a verb and a noun which, separately ('spear' as verb) or together, suggest action and force. As with the name of Fortinbras, literally 'strong-in-arm'.[21] This, then, would be the immediately remarkable thing: that the idea of what Derrida refers to as the third modality of the signature, 'the fold of the placement in abyss where ... the work of writing designates, describes, and inscribes itself as act (action and archive)' (*S*, 54), this idea is (banally) named in the name itself. Both as action (shaking, spearing, shaking a spear) and as archive (spear-shaking as flourish and as paraph): the name implies at once that which marks (a spear, like the stylus or other pointed objects which we shall consider in more detail below) and that which leaves no mark but only, perhaps, a trace — for this spear apparently does

not penetrate, it neither wounds nor even makes contact,
even though (or else precisely in so far as) the name comme-
morates an action, spear-shaking, which leaves no obvious
mark of itself.

'Shake hands' — as in sonnet 28, to seal a compact —
this is Shakespeare: no need, always other, impossible, it
won't have been his thing.

Dispersal and decomposition — the task of turning the
name, as Derrida puts it, 'into a blazon or legendary *rebus*'
(*S*, 60) might nevertheless be manifest in 'so many sigils, or
abbreviated, interrupted, and condensed signatures' (96), so
many signature-effects.[22] Let's start again, with Hamlet's first
encounter with the Ghost. This 'event' might be read as precisely a dramatisation of sealing/signing — from the opening
'Mark me' — 'I will' (I.v.2) — to the reportedly 'wild and
whirling words' used by Hamlet afterwards:

> And so, without more circumstance at all,
> I hold it fit that we shake hands and part:
> You, as your business and desire shall point you –
> For every man hath business and desire,
> Such as it is — and for my own poor part.... (I.v.127–31)

These lines supposedly tell nothing, like the Ghost's:

> But that I am forbid
> To tell the secrets of my prison-house,
> I could a tale unfold whose lightest word
> Would harrow up thy soul, freeze thy young blood,
> Make thy two eyes like stars start from their spheres,
> Thy knotted and combined locks to part,
> And each particular hair to stand an end
> Like quills upon the fretful porpentine.
> But this eternal blazon must not be
> To ears of flesh and blood. List, list, O list!
> If thou didst ever thy dear father love — (I.v.13–23)

Strange *occupatio* — saying without saying, marking by not
marking, remaining by disappearing, the strangest folding-
unfolding of all: signature or blazon in abyss. There is a certain
thickening in these lines, most clearly in 'Make ... stars
start ... spheres'; but an anticipation of the secret has perhaps been blurred together in Hamlet's prelude, his pledge of

attention in the Ghost's presence: '*Speak*; I am bound to *hear*' (I.v.6). And only to fall apart. For it is a question of the ear. Here, in the Ghost's speeches, one could trace all the sounds of 'e(a)r(e)' — right through to the critical injunction to 'Remember' and to the final repetitions of 'Swear'.

Leave the demonstration there, at least a moment, it will have already disappeared, as if into thin air. 'But soft, methinks I scent the morning air . . .' (I.v.58). A similar showing can be made for all the rhyming, miming and quasi-hallucinatory variants of 'shake/s'. A few instances, then, along with a few versions of '(sp)ear(e)', from a few lines of the remain-or-disappear, 'To be, or not to be' overheard soliloquy: 'heartache', 'shocks', 'heir', 'sleep', 'perchance', 'there's', 'shuffled', 'pause', 'there's', 'makes', 'bear', 'scorns', 'spurns', 'takes', 'make', 'bare', 'bear' (III.i.62–76), and so forth.

Who's there?

For it is a question of the ear — and of proper name and signature — from the first two words of *Hamlet* onwards. In the reading being advanced here, the significance of the ear in the play can no longer be confined merely to considerations of theme (poisoning, eavesdropping, etc.) or imagery ('the whisper', i.e. rumour, 'the whole ear of Denmark', etc.). Hamlet's response to hearing the Ghost lights the way: hearing must be supplemented by writing. In order to remember what he hears, Hamlet must 'set it down' (I.v.107) in writing. A notion of writing becomes decisive for the memorisation of what is heard; it thereby suggests itself as a necessary condition for acts of memory, hearing, speaking and even the so-called experience of self-presence. Writing commemoration. The 'ear', with all its more or less audible variants, is violently, uncontrollably caught up in signature and signature-effects.

Hence, from before the beginning, the (ex)-appropriateness of the manner of King Hamlet's death. This, together with a recurrent association of ear and specifically verbal poison (for example, III.ii.227–30; IV.v.88–91; IV.vii.101–4), might be used to initiate a demonstration of how the structure of the signature obeys a logic analogous to that of the *pharmakon* ('poison' as well as 'remedy', etc.) in Derrida's 'Plato's Pharmacy' (*D*, 61–171), not to mention that of the sponge.[23] Ear, wound, mark and name are repeatedly linked. They gather as folds and forms of signature. It may be a matter of listening for the impossible — and of glimpsing constellations of certain phonemes and graphemes, as in 'assail your ears' (I.i.34), 'with a hideous crash / Takes prisoner Pyrrus' ear' (II.ii.472–3), 'He would drown the stage with tears, / And cleave the general ear with horrid speech' (II.ii.556–7), 'A knavish speech sleeps in a foolish ear' (IV.ii.22–3), 'Will nothing stick our person to arraign / In ear and ear' (IV.v.93–4).

Or of hearing 'nothing but ourselves' (III.iv.135).

V

Signing: this is the fundamental (and fundamentally paradoxical) subject of *Hamlet*. What can hearing do? What kind of mark can sound leave?

> KING: How fares our cousin Hamlet?
> HAMLET: Excellent, i'faith, of the chameleon's dish. I eat the air, promise-cramm'd. You cannot feed capons so.
> KING: I have nothing with this answer, Hamlet. These words are not mine.
> HAMLET: No, nor mine now. — (III.ii.92–7)

On Hamlet's final retort, Harold Jenkins quotes Samuel Johnson: 'A man's words, says the proverb, are his own no longer than he keeps them unspoken' (Arden, 293). But writing, it should be clear, is scarcely different. Again and again *Hamlet* will focus on notions of proper sealing, proper signing — from the 'seal'd compact' (I.i.89) between Fortinbras and King Hamlet, which precedes the play, to the pharmaco-pharmaceutical compact between Laertes and Claudius ('Now must your conscience my acquittance seal . . .' (IV.vii.1)). The identification between Hamlet and Horatio moves at the level of names and seals — and what must not be forgotten:

> HAMLET: I am glad to see you well.
>   Horatio, or I do forget myself.
> HORATIO: The same, my lord, and your poor servant ever.
> HAMLET: Sir, my good friend, I'll change that name with you.
>   (I.ii.160–3)

Later, Hamlet will say, as near the ear as possible,

> Dost thou hear?
> Since my dear soul was mistress of her choice,
> And could of men distinguish her election,
> Sh'ath sealed thee for herself. (III.ii.62–5)

And this sealing seals the text — or rather opens the possibility of its being narrated. For it is only in accordance with the phantasmatic effectivity of this sealing that Horatio can be imagined capable of 'Truly deliver[ing]' (V.ii.391) an account of what happens. In the final transfer, in the midst of so much aphony, such polyphony, hearing is (impossibly) encrypted:

> If thou didst ever hold me in thy heart,
> Absent thee from felicity awhile,
> And in this harsh world draw thy breath in pain
> To tell my story. . . . (V.ii.351–4)

Hamlet comes right up to Horatio's ear, even in writing: 'I have words to speak in thine ear will make thee dumb; yet are they much too light for the bore of the matter . . . He that thou knowest thine, Hamlet' (IV.vi.22–8). But who wrote this? According to the first Sailor it was 'th'ambassador' (IV.vi.9). The question of the authenticity, propriety and properties of Hamlet's handwriting is raised more than once. 'Came this from Hamlet to her?' (II.ii.113), Gertrude asks, when Polonius is providing 'proof' of the nature of his 'madness'. And later, in response to the letter announcing Hamlet's 'sudden and more strange return', Laertes asks, 'Know you the hand?' — and the King avers: ''Tis Hamlet's character' (IV.vii.45–9). Criticism may variously inscribe the significance of Hamlet as a playwright — inside or outside the play? what play? neither in nor out, and both together as well? — and may variously assess which (if any) of Hamlet's 'dozen or sixteen lines' (II.ii.535) are inserted in *The Mousetrap*; but these ruminations stop short of the question of handwriting, the authenticity of 'character', seal or signature. How many plays does Hamlet write, and how many write Hamlet?

> Being thus benetted round with villainies —
> Or I could make a prologue to my brains,

> They had begun the play — I sat me down,
> Devis'd a new commission, wrote it fair —
> I once did hold it, as our statists do,
> A baseness to write fair, and labour'd much
> How to forget that learning, but, sir, now
> It did me yeoman's service. Wilt thou know
> Th'effect of what I wrote? (V.ii.29–37)

The play of writing precedes thought: without prologue, this play has already begun. Like Derrida's shopping list, handwriting is linked with forgetting.[24] Difficult to imagine a theory of autography without radical absence, forgetting, otherness, death — perhaps to precisely the degree that it is difficult to imagine the labour of *forgetting* how to write clearly and legibly ('fair'). And the nature of the handwriting here is crucial, like the nature of the seal: a matter of life and death.

A letter may not reach its destination; equally, it can kill. The letter which should have brought Hamlet's death brings the deaths of Rosencrantz and Guildenstern — thanks not only to Hamlet's unforgotten ability 'to write fair' but also to the seal or signature:

> HORATIO: How was this sealed?
> HAMLET: Why, even in that was heaven ordinant.
>   I had my father's signet in my purse,
>   Which was the model of that Danish seal,
>   Folded the writ up in the form of th'other,
>   Subscrib'd it, gave't th'impression, plac'd it safely,
>   The changeling never known. (V.ii.47–53)

Who signs and seals? And where? Monstrous impropriety and multiple divisions of the seal. Hamlet's signature, or subscription, is both proper and improper — and neither. 'That Danish seal' is, madly, both King Hamlet's and his murderer's; and Hamlet's 'model' (small copy or exact likeness) signs, undecidably, the internal ruptures and divisions of this seal.

How distinguish between Claudius and old Hamlet? Again, Hamlet invokes the idea of seals, characterising his father as

> A combination and a form indeed
> Where every god did seem to set his seal
> To give the world assurance of a man.
> This was your husband. Look you now what follows.

> Here is your husband, like a mildew'd ear
> Blasting his wholesome brother. . . . (III.iv.60–5)

Hamlet's father was a wholesome form covered with seals, and Claudius is 'a mildew'd ear'. Contrast or comparison? What is the status of 'assurance'? It is this last word which occurs again, in the graveyard scene:

> HAMLET: . . . Will his vouchers vouch him no more of his
>   purchases, and double ones too, than the length and
>   breadth of a pair of indentures? The very conveyances of
>   his lands will scarcely lie in this box, and must th'inheritor
>   himself have no more, ha?
> HORATIO: Not a jot, my lord.
> HAMLET: Is not parchment made of sheepskins?
> HORATIO: Ay, my lord, and of calveskins too.
> HAMLET: They are sheep and calves which seek out assurance
>   in that. . . . (V.i.106–15)

If 'assurance' (glossed by Jenkins as 'certainty of possession' and 'legal deed securing this' (Arden, 383)) is part of a play of signature, along with 'seek', 'parchment' and 'sheepskins', it is signature in abyss. What is the legitimacy or propriety of 'a pair of indentures'? Surely there is no point in writing. Writing is absurd. There is no permanence in it, no certainty of possession, either in or beyond itself, no possibility of proper monumentalisation. What can writing do? What kind of mark can a writer leave?

Ear, wound, mark and name: we come back to this chain. In doing so, we should underscore the suggestion that 'writing' be understood in a less narrow sense: just as it has an essential, as well as supplementary relation to the ear, to hearing and the voice, so it extends into the body and a supposedly extralinguistic world of action. Remember: wounding the ear — which is happening all the time — is inextricably linked up with the marking of the name. Words, 'spoken' as well as 'written', produce violent, 'material' effects. But we cannot any longer separate these fields — even if Hamlet seems to, for example, in reference to Gertrude:

> I will speak daggers to her, but use none.
> My tongue and soul in this be hypocrites:

> How in my words somever she be shent,
> To give them seals never my soul consent. (III.ii.387–90)

Any 'assurance' must deliquesce — at least once Hamlet '*Thrusts his rapier through the arras*' (III.iv.23), into 'the ear / Of all their conference' (to adopt Polonius's earlier description, in III.i.186–7), and once Gertrude 'repeats' (by what kind of uncanny machinery or dramaturgic telepathy?):[25]

> O speak to me no more.
> These words like daggers enter in my ears.
> No more, sweet Hamlet. (III.iv.94–6)

We will have to say that everything in *Hamlet* follows, in a circular or 'counter' (IV.v.110) fashion, from the idea of the 'wounded name' (V.ii.349), of telling it, telling its story, inscribing and monumentalising the name, producing 'wonder-wounded hearers' (V.i.250) and 'a living monument' (V.i.292). It is not only Hamlet, or Horatio, who is thus situated. All the doubling in the play feeds into this loop. Another 'double', Laertes, brings together 'voice' and wounded name, when he rejects Hamlet's request for pardon:

> ... but in my terms of honour
> I stand aloof, and will no reconcilement
> Till by some elder masters of known honour
> I have a voice and precedent of peace
> To keep my name ungor'd. (V.ii.242–6)

'But stay, what noise?' (IV.vii.161). The duel must come, even if — like the battle between Norway and Poland — it 'hath in it no profit but the name' (IV.iv.19).

Another 'double', Claudius, is also articulated on to the loop, inscribed in the ear-wound-mark-name chain. As when he calculates, for example,

> [So envious slander],
> Whose whisper o'er the world's diameter,
> As level as the cannon to his blank,
> Transports his poison'd shot, may miss our name
> And hit the woundless air. (IV.i.40–4)

A remark made by Derrida in *Spurs* may sharpen our reading and allow us to move it beyond *Hamlet*: 'In the question of style there is always the weight or *examen* of some pointed object. At times this object might be only a quill or a stylus. But it could just as easily be a stiletto, or even a rapier' (*Sp*, 37). The question of style — in so far as it is correlated with the idiomatic — will also shake down to the notion, and deposition, of a signature. Especially in the case (and chance) of a name like Shakespeare. It can be traced across the entire ever-'changeling' body of *Hamlet*, from the 'quills upon the fretful porpentine' to the 'treacherous instrument' (V.ii.322) which kills Hamlet, Laertes and Claudius. One must look for so many pointed objects — pins, partisans, swords, arrows, daggers, points, quills, bodkins. And above all, no doubt, as most provocative linking of the question of style and signature, the rapier. Signature-effects may seem to proliferate in those lines about the 'eyrie of children', for example, lines crucial to the dating of the play: 'These are now the fashion, and so berattle the common stages — so they call them — that many wearing rapiers are afraid of goose-quills and dare scarce come thither' (II.ii.339–42).[26] Almost as provocative, in their way, as the 'shak[ing] . . . parsnips' in the *Sir Thomas More Additions* (see *Riverside*, 1687).

But what is a signature? Who signs? How to sign, where and when? How to seal, how to monumentalise, how to leave a mark in or as writing? The validity of these questions is interdependent with that of the play's relentless exploration and questioning of death and mourning, memory and remembering, of the present and presence. Validity as legitimacy (questions of law and institutions) and as durability (questions also of monuments and monumentalisation). Everything in *Hamlet* which questions memory and self-presence is finally a question of (the impossibility of a proper) signing.[27]

All remembering is in the name of something.[28] In the Derrida–Ponge description, signing is associated with the notion of the wager and the duel.[29] *Hamlet* offers an elaboration of this association. It embraces yet exceeds all the forms of wager and compact in the play — for instance, between King Hamlet and King Fortinbras, Claudius and Gertrude, Polonius and Laertes and Ophelia, Hamlet and Horatio, Polonius and Reynaldo, Polonius and Claudius, Claudius and Fortin-

bras, Claudius and Gertrude and Rosencrantz and
Guildenstern, Hamlet and the Players ... It exceeds also the
singular compact between Hamlet and the Ghost Hamlet —
ostensibly sealed by the written 'word', 'Remember me', and
the swearing to silence by Hamlet's sword. It is, as such,
neither the duel between Hamlet and Laertes, nor the longer
one which has gone on between Hamlet and Claudius and to
which Hamlet refers when dismissing any guilt over the deaths
of Rosencrantz and Guildenstern: ''Tis dangerous when the
baser nature comes / Between the pass and fell incensed
points / Of mighty opposites' (V.ii.60–2). It is neither characterological, nor thematic, nor even an event. Rather *Hamlet*
is, from start to finish, the impossible dramatisation, deferral
and enactment, presentation, analysis and abyssing of the
signature.

Impossible because always other — and the other thing.
What will Shakespeare's thing have been? One might say the
ear, or Hamlet, or, with Hamlet, that 'The play's the thing'
(II.ii.600) or again 'The King is a thing' (IV.iii.27); one might
say 'woman', 'the Ghost', the ineptly-named 'Oedipus complex', the (even more laughable) 'objective correlative',
'memory', 'mourning'.... Any and all of these would only be
a way of seeming to bring close the impossible, the inaudible,
the unnamably other.

VI

What's in a name?

The preceding remarks and suggestions would furnish
a basis for the discussion and analysis of other putatively
'Shakespearean' texts. Circling in a gradual but determined
fashion back to the question of the remains of psychoanalysis
and the proper names of 'Freud' and 'Derrida', let us sketch
very rapidly some possible approaches to three other plays:
Romeo and Juliet, *Antony and Cleopatra* and *The Tempest*.

> O be some other name.
> What's in a name? That which we call a rose
> By any other word would smell as sweet;
> So Romeo would, were he not Romeo call'd,

> Retain that dear perfection, which he owes
> Without that title. (II.ii.42–7)

In 'Aphorism Countertime' Derrida offers an elaboration of Juliet's 'implacable analysis' (AC, 427) of the proper name here. He observes, for example, as follows:

> A proper name does not name anything which is human, which belongs to a human body, a human spirit, an essence of man. And yet this relation to the inhuman only befalls man, for him, to him, in the name of man. He alone gives himself this inhuman name. And Romeo would not be what he is, a stranger to his name, without this name. (AC, 427)

This 'noncoincidence and contretemps' (432) between the name and the bearer of the name is linked up, in Derrida's account, with the notion that *Romeo and Juliet* stages 'the theatre of the impossible', in which 'two people each outlive the other' (422). Within this theatre, Romeo and Juliet experience the impossible: 'Romeo dies before Juliet, whom he has seen dead. They both live, outlive the death of the other' (422). Such forms of (impossible) contretemps — the condition of every loving or identificatory rapport, suggests Derrida ('I love because the other is the other, because its time will never be mine': 420) — might also be exemplified in terms of the play's uneasy final confusion of monumentalisation and encrypting, rounding on names. This unease suggests, again, the impossibility of a proper signing. As though countersigning, *avant la lettre*, Juliet's 'O happy dagger. / This is thy sheath. There rust, and let me die' (V.iii.168–9), Romeo goes out with a paraph, shaking off inauspicious stars, calling for the impossible contract:

> O here
> Will I set up my everlasting rest
> And shake the yoke of inauspicious stars
> From this world-wearied flesh. Eyes, look your last.
> Arms, take your last embrace! And lips, O you
> The doors of breath, seal with a righteous kiss
> A dateless bargain to engrossing Death. (V.iii.109–15)

This bargain can be compared with Hamlet's 'quietus' (I.iii.75). 'Engrossing' means not only 'purchasing in gross, in large

quantities' or 'illegally monopolizing or amassing', but also
'writing a legal document' (Arden, 227): Death (capitalised
and capitalising as proper name) writes, and must
(impossibly) sign or 'seal' as well. Datelessness and monumentalisation. Unease through a multiplication of
monuments — the monument where Romeo and Juliet die,
the monument proposed to commemorate them, and the
monument entitled *Romeo and Juliet*. A question, finally, of
names and sealing a compact at any rate, in which the proper
name of Verona itself must participate:

> CAPULET: O brother Montague, give me thy hand.
> This is my daughter's jointure, for no more
> Can I demand.
> MONTAGUE: But I can give thee more,
> For I will raise her statue in pure gold,
> That whiles Verona by that name is known,
> There shall no figure at such rate be set
> As that of true and faithful Juliet.
> CAPULET: As rich shall Romeo's by his lady's lie,
> Poor sacrifices of our enmity. (V.iii.295–303)

Proper name and signature, monument and monumentalisation in *Antony and Cleopatra* require a reading of such con-
centration and subtlety that I can only give the most hesitant
of outlines. Space seems to close in.

Will you walk out of the air?

I have suggested that the ear, and a labyrinthine kind of
phone-book gathering around the sounds of 'e(a)r(e)', is a
signature-effect, and site of (impossible) sealing, in *Hamlet*.
The operation can be transferred to the air in *Antony and
Cleopatra*. One would have to listen to the ear as well, and to
those other kinds of signature-effect touched on in the discussion of *Hamlet*; but read also for a thread perhaps, for
knots of 'rare', 'yare', 'mare', 'chare' and so many more familiar others, leading to 'air'. Or not. Cleopatra is, says Antony,
'Like a right gipsy, that at fast and loose / Beguil'd me, to the
very heart of loss' (IV.xii.28–9). John Ingledew glosses 'fast
and loose' as follows: 'a game of deception formerly played
at fairs by gipsies. Having tied a knot in a belt or string, the
gipsy would get people to bet that it was real (*fast*), and would

then pull the two ends, removing the knot and showing that it was only an apparent one (*loose*)'.[30] Whether there is nothing, just air, or a knot, or not: the incipient hallucinosis of this alternative — if it is one — is tied to dissolution, air, signature, seal and death. In the power of its serenity and affirmation, Cleopatra's death may be breathtaking — like the resumption of an after-life, or living on — a trick or snare, or not, a knot. This mad suspension, between 'knot' and 'not', 'Shakespeare' and 'air', death and living on, and so on, is also caught by Caesar as he remarks on Cleopatra's corpse: 'she looks like sleep, / As she would catch another Antony / In her strong toil of grace' (V.ii.344–6). 'Toil' as 'net' or 'snare' (but not 'labour'?) goes back at least to Antony's entangling and sealing:

> Now all labour
> Mars what it does: yea, very force entangles
> Itself with strength: seal then, and all is done.
> Eros! — I come, my queen: — Eros! — Stay for me,
> Where souls do couch on flowers, we'll hand in hand,
> And with our sprightly port make the ghosts gaze. . . .
> (IV.xiv.47–52)

Antony's 'Stay' anticipates Cleopatra's final words, an aposiopoesis like a suspension in air, of mark and step: 'What should I stay — ' (V.ii.312). It lives on, undecidable, like an effect of fast and loose, or of the serpentine syntax of her preceding address to the asp: 'With thy sharp teeth this knot intrinsicate / Of life at once untie . . .' (V.ii.303–4).

Signsponge draws attention to ways in which the notions of signature and resolution are linked. There is irresolution in *Hamlet* — for rapid convenience call it structural, rather than characterological — and this would clearly complement the reading of *Hamlet* as a scene of signature. With *Antony and Cleopatra* resolution tends to be dissolution: dissolving, melting, discandying, vanishing. Not nothing; rather, transformation in and as 'air'. Hence the scattering of signature-effects, perhaps, in the clouds of Antony's lines:

> ANTONY: Eros, thou yet behold'st me?
> EROS: Ay, noble lord.
> ANTONY: Sometime we see a cloud that's dragonish,

>A vapour sometime, like a bear, or lion,
>A tower'd citadel, a pendent rock,
>A forked mountain, or blue promontory
>With trees upon 't, that nod unto the world,
>And mock our eyes with air. Thou hast seen these signs,
>They are black vesper's pageants.
>EROS: Ay, my lord.
>ANTONY: That which is now a horse, even with a thought
>The rack dislimns, and makes it indistinct
>As water is in water.
>EROS: It does, my lord.
>ANTONY: My good knave Eros, now thy captain is
>Even such a body. (IV.xiv.1–13)

And, with Cleopatra, the idea of some kind of appropriation of 'air' goes back to Enobarbus's early description:

>   From the barge
>A strange invisible perfume hits the sense
>Of the adjacent wharfs. The city cast
>Her people out upon her; and Antony,
>Enthron'd i' the market-place, did sit alone,
>Whistling to the air; which, but for vacancy,
>Had gone to gaze on Cleopatra too,
>And made a gap in nature. (II.ii.211–18)

At which impossible rarefaction, Agrippa exclaims 'Rare Egyptian!' And in the final scene Cleopatra will affirm: 'Husband, I come: / Now to that name, my courage prove my title! / I am fire, and air . . .' (V.ii.286–8). And again, twenty lines later:

>CHARMIAN: O, break! O, break!
>CLEOPATRA: As sweet as balm, as soft as air, as gentle.

What will 'air' be? What kind of thing? Perhaps both the 'vapour' of 'mechanic slaves / With greasy aprons, rules, and hammers' (V.ii.208–12) and 'power': signature and counter-signature of air and Shakes — paraph which is by the same gesture disappearance, vanishing; signature as, spongily, both dirt and 'perfection'; signature as entirely other, 'a gap in nature', death in short, and at the same time a monument of power. Shake. It is a question of a structure analogous to the logic of what Derrida terms *pas* (both 'not' and 'step'), which

we might render *knot-a-step*, or of an aposiopoesis which is at
the same time in some sense paraphonic:

> I saw her once
> Hop forty paces through the public street,
> And having lost her breath, she spoke, and panted,
> That she did make defect perfection,
> And, breathless, power breathe forth. (II.ii.228–32)

As with the mournful, airy power of the colossal imaging
of Antony, in Act V, scene ii (75ff.), it seems to be a question of
an impossible and absolutely singular sounding or voice, one
that could 'shake the orb' while being identified with 'all the
tuned spheres' (V.ii.84–5) . . .

A pair? — appear and disappear. How to round off,
embrace, clasp or name? 'No grave upon the earth shall clip
in it / A pair so famous' (V.ii.357–8).

Who's there?

Indeed, that is out o' th' air.

Can you hear lightning?

The Tempest begins with 'a tempestuous noise of thunder
and lightning heard' and in the midst of it, of so many waves,
in the first seventeen lines, the ghostly shapes of a signature
might be heard, like lightning, for instance in 'here', 'cheer',
'speak', 'yarely', 'bestir, bestir', 'cheerly, cheerly', 'yare, yare!',
'take', 'care', 'where', 'hear', 'mar our labour', a stressed
thread leading through to the Boatswain's 'Hence! What cares
these roarers for the name of King?' (I.i.16–17). Or knot. The
name is here, in *The Tempest*, as both 'roar' and (musical)
'air'. Are you awake?

'Shake it off. Come on' (I.ii.309).

The Tempest's concern with the power of language is a
concern with the hypnotic power of sound. It is a matter of
the relations between hypnosis, drama and poetry, in other
words of a hypnopoetics.

No need to repeat the numerous arguments for seeing
Prospero as a figure of the playwright or the text as an allegory
of 'the story' of Shakespeare's life. Our only interest here
would be in the name, the signature, the William-Shakespeare-
text. Everything in the text is to be heard — right 'To th'syll-

able' (I.ii.504) — and everything will come down to the name.
Between the impropriety and violence of the 'roar' and the
clear, formal beauty of the (musical) 'air'; or rather, passing
through them. Or knot.

The *OED* defines 'paronomasia' as 'a playing on words
which sound alike; a word-play; a pun'. It specifies its deri-
vation from the Greek verb παρονομαζειν, 'to alter slightly
in naming'; but warns against confusing it with another word,
'prosonomasia' which is, 'properly, a calling by a name, a nickna-
ming', and derives from the Greek προσονομαζειν, 'to call by
a name'. We promise to try not to confuse them, or make a
paronymous botch of them, properly speaking. Nevertheless it is
clear that the names of Miranda (see I.ii.428–31, and III.i.36–8)
and Caliban (as cannibal or otherwise deformed, to the syllable,
as ''Ban, 'Ban, Cacaliban', at II.ii.184) traverse both terms —
not to mention that of Prospero (there seems to be play on
'prosper', for example, at II.i.69, II.ii.2, and IV.i.104). For the
name 'Prospero' is also a paronomasia of the proper name of
Shakespeare, and even of the 'proper' itself. Prosperonomasia:
'Prospero' as (impossibly proper) signature-effect.

Shake off slumber, and beware:
    Awake, Awake!
                    (II.i.299–300)

Ariel too — that spirit 'which art but air' (V.i.21) and which, by
the most lightening paronomasia, carries the air in its name . . .

What is fascinating, or spell-binding, is the (impossible)
chance of saying the name, not only of letting the name be signed
or inscribed in the text, in accordance with some of the kinds of
signature-effects so far indicated, but also of letting *The Tempest*
finally say nothing at all except the name. Between 'Prospero'
and 'Ariel', 'roar' and 'air', the dramatisation of the signature as
sound — as something holy, majestic, monumental.

But can it be heard? Are you awake? For instance, in these
exchanges:

ALONSO: Wherefore this ghastly looking?
GONZALO: What's the matter?
SEBASTIAN: Whiles we stood here securing your repose,
    Even now, we heard a hollow burst of bellowing
    Like bulls, or rather lions: did't not wake you?
    It struck mine ear most terribly.

> ALONSO: I heard nothing.
> ANTONIO: O, 'twas a din to fright a monster's ear,
>   To make an earthquake! sure, it was the roar
>   Of a whole herd of lions.
> ALONSO: Heard you this, Gonzalo?
> GONZALO: Upon mine honour, sir, I heard a humming,
>   And that a strange one too, which did awake me:
>   I shak'd you, sir, and cried.... (II.ii.304–14)

One might hear Shakespeare, nothing, a roar, or 'humming' air.
Or knot. Frank Kermode glosses the lines about the bellowing,
earthquaking sound as 'Possibly in allusion to the many
accounts of terrifying noises on unexplored islands, from
Hanno up to date' (Arden, 60). Perhaps; but more obvious is
the way in which the hearing of this sound anticipates Alonso's experience in Act III:

> GONZALO: I' th' name of something holy, sir, why stand you
>   In this strange stare?
> ALONSO: O, it is monstrous, monstrous!
>   Methought the billows spoke, and told me of it;
>   The winds did sing it to me; and the thunder,
>   That deep and dreadful organ-pipe, pronounc'd
>   The name of Prosper.... (III.iii.95–9)

Difficult to hear in all the noise. Wake up still in sleep.
Where should this music be? The trees are toppling.

The power of sound, the musical forces of language: these
constitute the spell within and of the play, crossing and
recrossing the borders to form a singular, multiple knot.
Knotty oak and arms:

> [I have] 'twixt the green sea and the azur'd vault
> Set roaring war: to the dread rattling thunder
> Have I given fire, and rifted Jove's stout oak
> With his own bolt; the strong-bas'd promontory
> Have I made shake, and by the spurs pluck'd up
> The pine and cedar: graves at my command
> Have wak'd their sleepers.... (V.i.43–9)

This extraordinary paraph coincides with the abjuration of
rough magic: a kind of disappearing in order to remain. Being
'bound up' (I.ii.489), 'knit up' (III.iii.89), in 'bondage' (III.i.41)
– this is all undone ('Untie the spell', says Prospero at V.i.253),

only in order that the other begins, already will have begun.
A knot. Or not.

> It is a sleepy language, and thou speak'st
> Out of thy sleep. . . .
>
> (II.i.206–7)

What happens? Will all have 'melted into air, into thin air'
(IV.i.150) — fast and loose.

By me, William Shakespeare.

VII

Appalled by his disregard, by the fact that he didn't seem to
give a damn about his plays, about having them properly
written down, edited or printed, Delia Bacon supposed that
Shakespeare must have 'cared for them precisely as a trades-
man would — cared for them as he would have cared for tin
kettles, or earthen pans and pots, if they had been in his line,
instead'.[31] That will do, in part: a line in ordinary, common
objects.

While greasy Joan doth keel the pot. . . . [32] Greasy aprons,
rules, and hammers. The thin air of things. Dissolves into
insignificance. After all, to adopt Derrida's words, the question
of the name is never more 'than a little, insignificant piece of
the whole corpus. And [the poet's] work is so little the product of his name that it springs rather from an aptitude for
doing without it' (S, 116).

One or two final threads of insignificance to pick out here,
which may turn out to be one or more, to close, or not.

First thread. Derrida writes: 'To signify oneself in the insignificant (outside meaning or concept), isn't this the same
thing as signing?' (S, 40). One might pursue this question
through an analysis of what is classically recognised as a
mark of Shakespeare's 'greatness': his facility for engaging
with, for representing the ordinary, the insignificant or obvious. And, suggestively in accordance with Derrida's formulation of 'style', a facility for this facility itself: 'easie numbers'
(as Milton's poem has it) — a style which appears to advance
in advance, weaving (itself) away, throwing off (everything in)
its path (that is to say, precisely, *the obvious*), like just so
much insignificance, not worth a jot.[33]

Second thread. The notion of marking the insignificant might be thought in terms of being resolute. Lacan empha- sises the idea of the duel in *Hamlet* and how the objects offered in the wager ('six Barbary horses' against 'six French rapiers and poniards, with their assigns, as girdle, hanger, and so' (V.ii.144–7)) take on 'the character of what is called a *vanitas* in the religious tradition'. The notion of signature might then affect the context and sense of Lacan's observation that Hamlet 'stakes his resolution against the things that interest him least in the world, and he does so to win for someone else'.[34] Marking both the insignificant and the *objet a*.[35] This can be generalised: doesn't work on signature and signature-effects open up the possibility of a redescription, a transformation of the very grounds, of psychoanalysis, of the concepts of 'ego' and 'narcissism', 'identification' and 'trans- ference', and of the entire (insignificant) psychopathology of everyday life?

Not forgetting the forgetting of proper names, not least that of Freud, the Freudian slip, the slip or slip-knot of 'Freud'. . . .

One has to try the argument out on various people, but Arnold Zweig proves stubborn. Enthusing about Edward de Vere, Freud writes to Zweig in 1937: 'I do not know what still attracts you to the man of Stratford . . . It almost irritates me that you should support the notion.'[36] Nearly a year earlier, anticipating a visit from Zweig, Freud had written: 'You must bring Looney back with you. I must try him on others, for obviously with you I have had no success.'[37] Does this remind us of anything?

A month earlier, in May 1936, this time to Stefan Zweig: 'For with the biographer as with the psychoanalyst we find phenomena which come under the heading of "trans- ference".'[38]

Analysts have been embarrassed about Freud's involve- ment in the Bacon–Shakespeare controversy; it is seen as a curious aberration, perhaps best forgotten, comparable to his involvement with the question of telepathy. Yes, let's try to forget about it.

Or knot. In which case wouldn't this curious aberration operate according to the logic of what Derrida in another context calls an 'unanalysed remainder' (*PC*, 519)? Then far from being an eccentric or whimsical concern out on the margins of Freud's thought, the Bacon–Shakespeare controversy and all that it entails would be alive and stirring at the heart of the inside. Like 'telepathy', and like 'hypnosis' too.[39] In various and interconnected ways, all three — hypnosis, telepathy, the Bacon–Shakespeare controversy — would lead us to focus on notions of a radical alterity, fictionality and literarity. All three might thus also be seen to figure the concealed and unacknowledgeable distractions of 'distraction' itself, within the conceptuality and the historical emergence of psychoanalysis.

The Bacon–Shakespeare controversy as the distraction of 'Freud': as with 'telepathy', what is at issue here is a foreign body or an encrypting.[40] Implanted, engendered by 'Shakespeare'. What could this mean? *Hamlet*-signed. Freud's suspicions were aroused by the name of Delia Bacon; perhaps it is less strange that he appeared not to see, in the letters of the name 'de Vere' (and even the alternative, 'Oxford'), a scattered projection of his own name. In any case, psychoanalysis is situated as a discourse engulfed and haunted by an anxiety (even a kind of onomatopathology) regarding the signature and proper name — by a refusal or an inability, among other things to sign, countersign or be signed by, 'literature'. 'Literature' here can be defined as the discourse which, more rigorously perhaps than any other, concerns itself with the impossibility of signing, with the radical anonymity of writing and with the entirely other by which its space and chances are opened.[41]

VIII

But what if Looney and his disciple Freud were correct after all, and the author really was de Vere? Wouldn't that name function just as satisfactorily in producing supposed signature-effects of 'ear' and 'air'?

Or perhaps Leonardo, the existence of whose 'Academia Vinciana' Freud doubted — an institution, as Freud pointed out, 'postulated from the existence of five or six emblems' (*PFL*,14: 222). In a footnote he quotes Giorgio Vasari:

[Leonardo] lost some time by even making a drawing of knots of cords, in which it was possible to trace the thread from one end to the other until it formed a completely circular figure. A very complex and beautiful design of this sort is engraved on copper; in the middle can be read the words 'Leonardus Vinci Academia'. (*PFL*,14: 222, n.1)

Notes

1 See Ernest Jones, *Sigmund Freud: Life and Work*, vol. III (London: Hogarth Press, 1957), 419, 462. Further references to the biography will be given in the text, preceded by 'Jones' where appropriate.

2 In the present chapter, references to the works customarily attributed to 'Shakespeare' are based on the following Arden editions: *Hamlet*, ed. Harold Jenkins (London: Methuen, 1982), *Romeo and Juliet*, ed. Brian Gibbons (London: Methuen, 1980), *Antony and Cleopatra*, ed. M. R. Ridley (London: Methuen, 1954; rpt 1981) and *The Tempest*, ed. Frank Kermode (London: Methuen, 1954; rev. rpt 1979). Where appropriate, page references to these editions are preceded by 'Arden' in the text. Where possible, other references to Shakespeare and related material are taken from the *Riverside Shakespeare* (hereafter *Riverside*), ed. G. Blakemore Evans et al. (Boston: Houghton Mifflin, 1974).

3 Samuel Schoenbaum, *Shakespeare's Lives* (Oxford: Clarendon Press, 1970), 529–629. Further page references are given in the text. For another and more recent account of the Bacon–Shakespeare controversy, especially from a more literary theoretical perspective, see Marjorie Garber, *Shakespeare's Ghost Writers: Literature as Uncanny Causality* (London: Methuen, 1987), esp. 1–27.

4 See Schoenbaum, 591ff.

5 Thus at the end of a hundred pages of scrupulous documentation, Schoenbaum cannot refrain from interposing: 'Perhaps at this pause in the narrative the writer may be permitted to drop for a moment the historian's mask of impersonality and give vent to private emotion. This section ["Deviations"] has been the cruelest assignment I have ever confronted. The sheer volume ... appals ...' (627).

6 Harry Trosman, 'Freud and the Controversy over Shakespearean Authorship', *Journal of the American Psychoanalytic Association*, 13:3 (July 1965): 475–98. Further page references are given in the main body of the text.

7 See Trosman, 481.

8 See, in particular, 'To Speculate — on "Freud" ' (*PC*, 257–409).

9 In this way we might then reconsider: what, essentially, is anti-
   Stratfordian discourse? It is an engagement with the question and
   power of the proper name. Schoenbaum's 'Deviations' seems repeatedly to verge on a recognition of this, on the decisiveness and
   essentiality of naming — but without naming it as such. Shakespeare's name as the one to conjure, to juggle with, all the time, but
   also the proper names of the anti-Stratfordians themselves: J.
   Thomas Looney, Sherwood E. Silliman and George M. Battey, for
   instance. 'How innocently appropriate are some anti-Stratfordian
   names!' exclaims Schoenbaum (625). The question of what is 'inno-
   cent' or 'appropriate', we would note, is necessarily bound up with
   notions of the illegitimate, the proper and improper. Throughout
   anti-Stratfordian writings, it is a matter of the appropriations, the
   property and propriety of proper names. And always also expropri-
   ation, the non-proper, the improper. The title, the name of the author
   and the thesis of one anti-Stratfordian study dramatises this with a
   certain hilarity: *Our Elusive Willy: A Slice of Concealed Elizabethan
   History*, by Ira Sedgwick Proper, which argues that William Seymour,
   illegitimate son of the Earl of Hertford and Lady Catherine Grey, was
   christened as 'William Shakespeare'. If Schoenbaum recounts this
   (613) in a perfectly 'proper' and 'sober' fashion, he treats *Wie was
   Shakespeare*, by F. Louise W. M. Buisman-de Savornin Lohman, a
   little more directly: 'the most remarkable feature of this effort, if
   one may judge from the English summary graciously appended, is
   the name of the authoress' (616). But Schoenbaum's stress on names
   is largely inadvertent, clearly subordinate to more 'fundamental'
   considerations of scholarly exposition, commentary and judgment.
   A slight drawing apart, displacement or deviation, however, and
   'Deviations' might be readily articulated on to a critical analysis of
   proper names, a deconstructive meditation on the institutional and
   monumental significance of the proper name of Shakespeare. What
   Celeston Demblon called '*l'ex-boucher stratfordien*' (cited by Schoenbaum, 619) might become a kind of *lex-bouchon*, a reading-stopper,
   the distraction of a traffic-jam or catastrophic pile-up around the
   reading of a name.

10 See William F. Friedman and Elizebeth S. Friedman, *The Shakespearean Ciphers Examined: An Analysis of Cryptographic Systems
   Used as Evidence that Some Author Other than William Shakespeare
   Wrote the Plays Commonly Attributed to Him* (Cambridge: Cambridge
   University Press, 1957). The Friedmans' concern is to show how
   'claims based on cryptography can be scientifically examined, and
   proved or disproved' (xv). Thus before coming to reject the arguments for the use of a biliteral cipher, for example, they carefully
   establish what we might call a necessary undecidability: 'For even
   if a claim to authorship were found in the First Folio, using Bacon's

biliteral cipher, this in itself would not be conclusive. The message could have been inserted by the printer himself, playing an elaborate hoax on posterity' (92).

11 *The Shakespearean Ciphers Examined*, 280.

12 Samuel Schoenbaum, *Internal Evidence and Elizabethan Dramatic Authorship: An Essay in Literary History and Method* (Evanston, Illinois: Northwestern University Press, 1966), 218.

13 Richard Rand, 'Greenwood', in *Signéponge/Signsponge* (*S*), xi.

14 The phrase 'taking chances' alludes to the collection of essays, *Taking Chances: Derrida, Psychoanalysis, and Literature*, eds Joseph H. Smith and William Kerrigan (London: Johns Hopkins University Press, 1984), especially Derrida's own contribution, 'My Chances / Mes Chances: A Rendezvous with Some Epicurean Stereophonies', 1–32. For another essay specifically concerned with 'science' and 'belief', see 'No Apocalypse, Not Now (full speed ahead, seven missiles, seven missives)' (NA).

15 Richard Rand, in the discussion following his 'o'er-brimm'd', in the *Oxford Literary Review*, 5 (1982), 55.

16 James Joyce, *Ulysses* (Harmondsworth: Penguin, 1974), 188–9.

17 *Ulysses*, 209. For another account of Shakespeare, *Hamlet* and (the ghostliness of) naming, see Maud Ellmann's 'The Ghosts of *Ulysses*', in *The Languages of Joyce*, eds R. M. Bollettieri Bosinelli, C. Marengo Vaglio and C. Van Boheemen (Amsterdam and Philadelphia: John Benjamins, 1992), 103–19.

18 See T, 7. For a recent and characteristically energetic cultural materialist account of the Shakespeare monument in this context, see Terence Hawkes, *Meaning by Shakespeare* (London and New York: Routledge, 1992).

19 Derrida distinguishes what he calls 'three modalities of signature' (*S*, 52). The first is 'The one that we call the signature in the proper sense ... the act of someone ... engaged in authenticating (if possible) the fact that it is indeed he who writes: here is my name, I refer to myself, named as I am, and I do so, therefore, in my name. I, the undersigned, I affirm (yes, on my honor)' (52, 54). The second is 'the set of idiomatic marks that a signer might leave by accident or intention in his product' and which have 'no essential link with the form of the proper name as articulated or read "in" a language': this is what is often called 'the style, the inimitable idiom of a writer, sculptor, painter, or orator' (54). The third and most enigmatic is designated 'as general signature, or signature of the signature' (54): it might be described as a kind of writerliness or self-referentiality which is able to efface itself, thus ensuring that 'it is the other, the

thing as other, that signs' (54). *Signsponge* is concerned to explore the singularity with which the Francis-Ponge-text combines all three modalities.

20 Cf. *JD i*, 180ff.

21 See Arden *Hamlet*, 163. Etymologically, of course, the spear marks many names, among them Roger ('fame-spear'), Oscar ('god-spear'), Edgar ('happy-spear'), Gerald ('spear-wielding'), Gerard ('spear-hard'), Gervase ('spear-servant') and — since *Hamlet* beckons — Gertrude ('spear-might').

22 Cf. Richard Rand's remark of Wordsworth's poetry: 'there are many, many places, in "Tintern Abbey" and in "Michael" for instance, where the language develops a certain thickness and all the graphemes and phonemes of the name William Wordsworth suddenly begin to fulminate. It's not accidental. The letters are scattered, dispersed like the body of Orpheus' (*Oxford Literary Review*, 5 (1982), 55).

23 The sponge, in Derrida's account of Ponge, figures the very (im)possibility of the signature. The weird character of the sponge as both proper (clean, dry) and improper (soiled, wet), both itself (empty) and other (full of what is not itself), is evoked by Hamlet's 'knavish speech' to the sponges called Rosencrantz and Guildenstern: 'When [the King] needs what you have gleaned, it is but squeezing you and, sponge, you shall be dry again' (IV.ii.18–20). Ned Lukacher has also noted the relation between the poisoning of Hamlet's father and Shakespeare's signature: 'The manner of the crime is in effect Shakespeare's own signature in the play, the inimitable mark of his originality. With the ear-poisoning, Shakespeare signs his text twice, once as the author on the title page and again, in a kind of antonomasia, by dismantling his proper name into the common nouns that compose it: ShakespEARE' (*Primal Scenes: Literature, Philosophy, Psychoanalysis* (Ithaca: Cornell University Press, 1986), 227). Lukacher does not, however, elaborate on the strange logic of this signature-effect.

24 The apparent need for Hamlet to write down the Ghost's 'word', in Act I, scene v, may correspondingly be illuminated by Derrida's example of the shopping list: '*At the very moment* "I" make a shopping list, I know (I use "knowing" here as a convenient term to designate the relations that I necessarily entertain with the object being constructed) that it will only be a list if it implies my absence, if it already detaches itself from me in order to function beyond my "present" act and if it is utilizable at another time, in the absence of my-being-present-now, even if this absence is the simple "absence of memory" that the list is meant to make up for, shortly, in a moment, but one which is already the following moment, the

absence of the now of writing, of the writer maintaining [*du mainten-ant-écrivant*], grasping with one hand his ballpoint pen. Yet no matter how fine this point may be, it is like the *stigmè* of every mark, already split. The sender of the shopping list is not the same as the receiver, even if they bear the same name and are endowed with the identity of a single ego. Indeed, were this self-identity or self-presence as certain as all that, the very idea of a shopping list would be rather superfluous or at least the product of a curious compulsion. Why would I bother about a shopping list if the presence of sender to receiver were so certain?' (LI, 49).

25 For a more detailed account of the notion of dramaturgic telepathy, see the reading of *Antony and Cleopatra* in my *Telepathy and Literature: Essays on the Reading Mind* (Oxford and Cambridge, Mass.: Blackwell, 1991), 142–59.

26 See Jenkins's notes in Arden, 25–6, 470–2; and for the notion of dating as itself a form of signing, see Derrida's 'Shibboleth' (Sh).

27 For a somewhat different account of memory and the present in *Hamlet*, permit me to refer to my 'Nuclear Piece: *Mémoires* of *Hamlet* and the Time to Come', *Diacritics*, 20:1 (spring 1990), 39–55. See too Derrida's *Spectres de Marx: L'Etat de la dette, le travail du deuil et la nouvelle Internationale* (Paris: Galilée, 1993), which offers an extended reading of Hamlet's 'The time is out of joint' (I.v.196) in terms of the disjointedness, the disjunctions and dislocations of the present *with itself*.

28 For an account of the ways in which 'We cannot separate the name of "memory" and "memory" of the name; we cannot separate the name and memory', see Derrida's *Mémoires* (*M*), 49 and passim.

29 In *Signsponge* too, we should note, this strange 'duel' must 'carry on to the death' (*S*, 14). It is a question of the impossible (mute) challenge of what Derrida calls 'the thing' — that is to say, the 'entirely other' (12) — and of a law of debt and forfeit which is indeed 'more than life-long' (70).

30 *Antony and Cleopatra*, ed. John Ingledew (Harlow, Essex: Longman, 1983), 158.

31 Cited by Schoenbaum, 535.

32 This is the refrain with which *Love's Labour's Lost* closes: see V.ii.920, 929 (*Riverside*, 212).

33 See *Spurs* (*Sp*), 39 and passim.

34 Jacques Lacan, 'Desire and the Interpretation of Desire in Hamlet', trans. James Hulbert, in *Yale French Studies*, 55/56 (1977): 30.

35 In this way we might be drawn to reconsider, for example, Lacan's analysis of the appearance of the skull in Holbein's 'The Ambassa-

dors'. Lacan notes that 'This picture is simply what any picture is, a trap for the gaze. In any picture, it is precisely in seeking the gaze in each of its points that you will see it disappear' (*The Four Fundamental Concepts of Psycho-Analysis*, ed. Jacques-Alain Miller, trans. Alan Sheridan (London: Hogarth Press and the Institute of Psycho-Analysis, 1977), 89). The anamorphic skull in this painting offers us, according to Lacan, 'the imaged embodiment of the *minus-phi* [- φ] of castration' (89): we might additionally, or rather, wish to trace its figuring of hollow bone (*hohl bein*). (I would like to record my indebtedness for this observation to the late Cyril Hall.)

36 *The Letters of Sigmund Freud & Arnold Zweig*, ed. Ernst L. Freud, trans. Prof. and Mrs. W. D. Robson-Scott (London: Hogarth Press and the Institute of Psycho-Analysis, 1970), 140.

37 *The Letters of Sigmund Freud & Arnold Zweig*, 132.

38 *Letters of Sigmund Freud 1873–1939*, ed. Ernst L. Freud, trans. Tania and James Stern (London: Hogarth Press, 1961), 426.

39 As regards the question of hypnosis, we might attend to the emphasis given, in the remarkable work of Mikkel Borch-Jacobsen, to its constitutive and ineffaceable role in the institution of psychoanalysis; and in particular to the way in which hypnosis comes back, in ghostly fashion, to the centre-stage of Freud's later work. See Borch-Jacobsen, *The Freudian Subject*, trans. Catherine Porter (London: Macmillan, 1989), and the more recent collection of essays entitled *The Emotional Tie: Psychoanalysis, Mimesis, and Affect*, trans. Douglas Brick and others (Stanford, California: Stanford University Press, 1992), especially the essays entitled 'Hypnosis in Psychoanalysis' (39–61) and 'Talking Cure' (75–97). In 'Hypnosis in Psychoanalysis', Borch-Jacobsen observes: 'Psychoanalysis no doubt did found itself on the abandonment of hypnosis — but only, it must be recognized, to see hypnosis reappear, sometimes under other names or in other forms, at the crossroads of all questions; hence, the importance of reconsidering this so-called abandonment, not so much to initiate a "return to hypnosis" as to examine, in light of the questions Freud was asking himself in his last phase, the reasons why in his first phase he had believed, rather too quickly, that these issues were settled. In other words, what is important is to reconsider what Freud called the "prehistory" of psychoanalysis, to return to it with the suspicion that this "prehistory" belongs to a certain future of psychoanalysis rather than to a long-dead past' (*The Emotional Tie*, 44).

40 As regards what puts the Bacon–Shakespeare controversy in touch with the question of telepathy, let us merely add here the hypothesis that it would be difficult to imagine a theory of telepathy (in the traditional sense of that term) which would not involve, as a quasi-essential condition, the identification of a (so-called) proper name. In this context

we might recall the suggestive anecdote recounted by Ernest Jones, in the chapter on 'Occultism': 'Ferenczi was now getting venturesome. Seeing a soldier in a tramcar he made a guess at his name and as they got out asked him, "Are you Herr Kohn?" The astonished man answered in the affirmative. Freud found the story "uncannily beautiful", but could not attribute it to telepathy because the man could hardly be expected to carry a visual picture of his name about with him. He said afterwards, however, that he was impressed by Ferenczi's argument that a man's name was a sensitive area and thus could more easily be communicated to a stranger' (III, 415).

41 In this way it would perhaps have less to do with Derrida's conception of literature as an institution 'which in principle allows one to say everything' (TSICL, 36), and more to do with the notion of a space in which one cannot say anything with any assurance at all *in one's name*, under one's name, in the juridically assurable name of *any one*. (I consider this definition of that 'strange institution called literature' in further detail below, in particular in Chapter 8.) Such a distinction might also point towards what is in certain respects, I think, a problematic characteristic of Derrida's work in this context, *viz.* that — while his texts *engage* the literary through their relentless demonstrations of the impossibility of signing, the exappropriation of the proper name, and so on — they nevertheless frequently draw attention to their authorship, making this authorship (as for instance in 'Signature Event Context' (SEC) or 'Limited Inc' (LI) or more recently 'Circumfession' (*JD ii*)) an explicit fact or theme, even if a primary effect of the text in question is to deconstruct the assumptions on which the identity and authority of such authorship rely. At stake here are important questions about the authority-effects perhaps inevitably courted and/or generated by a critico-theoretical analysis of the signature and proper name (such as Derrida's work furnishes) when the example for that analysis is the author of the analysis. Cf. Peggy Kamuf's remarks in a footnote in her *Signature Pieces: On the Institution of Authorship* (Ithaca: Cornell University Press, 1988), 4–5, n.5, where she discusses the dissemination of Derrida's signature in various texts. Kamuf here likewise poses the question of 'what happens when that signature [Derrida's] is cited, as it is here [in *Glas* and elsewhere], to back up claims being made about signatures in general' (5).

6

Philosophy and the ruins of deconstruction

'A title is always a promise' (*M*, 115). The title is already, here and now, decapitated.

This chapter, the possibility of the chapter in general, is caput. What you have here are a few aphorisms, bits of postcards and other fragments. On the *philo-* of philosophy and deconstruction.

'By what right are these aphorisms, these sententious fragments, or these poetic flashes linked together — ?' (PSAWV, 289), asks Derrida, but I cut him off, I'm leaving the quotation as it stands, a fragment, a ruin.

The preface, the institution, the dialectic, spirit, being — in ruins.

Philosophy is the ruination of deconstruction; deconstruction leaves philosophy in ruins. These ruins can never amount to being circular.

Deconstruction is volcanic.

If Derrida's work does or adds something to philosophy, this surely happens not only in the form of a critical supplement (by which it is demonstrated that deconstruction, like the supplement, is at the origin; philosophy is always already in deconstruction, deconstruction does not come *after* philosophy, etc.) but also in terms of a kind of unprecedented rapport with the literary, the dramatic and poetic. There will, one hopes, always be studies of Derrida, studies *after* Derrida (following Derrida, in the manner of Derrida, succeeding Derrida) which — like, for example, Rodolphe Gasché's *The Tain of the Mirror*[1] or Geoffrey Bennington's 'Derridabase' (*JD i*) — expound and elaborate Derrida's thought in what might be described as quite traditional philosophical terms, even if

that exposition and elaboration comprises (as it does, perhaps, in the case of Bennington's work) a deconstruction of
the systematicity of any and every 'systematic' philosophy.
But, alongside the quite proper and necessary concerns for
explanation and elucidation, any writing 'after Derrida' is also
called upon to render or countersign that which can provisionally be named 'literary', 'dramatic', 'poetic' in Derrida's
texts, and in particular their formal inventiveness, tonal dis-
locutionariness, telepathic interruptiveness in relation to traditional philosophical writing.[2]

This, then, is an essay on and in the ruination of the philosophical essay.

One could isolate a number of Derridean aphorisms: 'A title
is always a promise', 'There is nothing outside context' (ATED,
136), 'The referent is in the text' (DA, 19), 'Translation is
necessary but impossible' (DTB, 170, 174), 'Deconstruction
is *plus d'une langue* — both more than a language and no
more of *a* language' (see *M*, 15), 'The law is mad' (LG, 251),
and so on. If this helps to suggest the extent to which Derrida's
'style' can be thought about as aphoristic, it would also be
necessary to take account of what he has to say about aphorism as such. Aphorisms may indeed turn out to be 'irremediably edifying' (FTA: no.42), and the desire for aphorism may
be, in some sense, the philosophical desire *par excellence*,
viz. the desire for being able to '[say] the truth in the form
of the last judgment' (AC, 418); but Derrida's work entails, at
the same time, a critical, philosophical decomposition and
transformation of aphorism itself. Derrida insists on the gen-
eric and formal specificity of the aphorism while deforming
its limits — for instance in the text entitled 'Fifty-Two Aphorisms for a Foreword', starting with its very title and the corollary proposition that 'There is a genre forbidden to the
preface, it is the aphorism' (FTA: no.20); or with the sectioning
of 'Aphorism Countertime' (AC), in which it is no longer certain where the aphoristic stops and starts. In ways that closely
correspond to the practice of fragment-writing characteristic
of the *Athenaeum*, as analysed by Maurice Blanchot and by
Philippe Lacoue-Labarthe and Jean-Luc Nancy, Derrida elaborates a theory and practice of aphorism as double-bind, para-

doxy, impossibility.[3] Thus, for Derrida, there is a kind of double-bind that characterises the very identity of an aphorism: 'an aphorism . . . is sufficient unto itself' (FTA: no.24), but 'There is always more than one aphorism' (FTA: no.45). Or as he puts it in 'Aphorism Countertime', 'an aphorism never arrives by itself, it doesn't come all alone. It is part of a serial logic' (AC, 416). If the paradoxy of aphorism is perhaps most succinctly, or most aphoristically, propounded in Aphorism 21 of 'Fifty-Two Aphorisms' — 'This is not an aphorism' — the negativity of such a definition requires circumspection. An aphorism is and is not itself.

Not least because of its linkage with a proper name (unlike a proverb, which may be anonymous), aphorism is at once necessary and impossible (cf. AC, 433).[4] The proper name of the aphorist both belongs and does not belong to the aphorism. An aphorism ought to be readable alone, by itself, the expression of a truth which does not depend on the certificating assignation of an author, and yet . . .

Strikingly, at least in 'Aphorism Countertime' and 'Fifty-Two Aphorisms', Derrida does not devote attention to the name of the *aphorist*. One might say that he diverts it, instead, in the direction of the notion of the aphorism as a name and of the name in general *as aphorism*.

'Aphorism' is itself a name, an entitling or genre-clause, which does not simply belong to what it names.

Philosophy is an aphorism.

But there is no aphorism, and therefore no philosophy, without engaging with the poetic.

There is a rhetorical figure incompatible with the aphorism: it is aposiopoesis. Yet every aphorism — in its very provocation, in its elliptical or sententious character — is pervaded by the aposiopoetic.

In so far as it both is and is not sufficient unto itself, an aphorism is at once ruin and monument. A corresponding logic applies also to aphorisms presented in a series, as if in the form of a self-contained text (entitled, for example,

'Aphorism Countertime' or, perhaps, 'Philosophy and the Ruins of Deconstruction'). As Derrida puts it: 'Despite their fragmentary appearance, [aphorisms] make a sign towards the memory of a totality, at the same time ruin and monument' (FTA: no.46).

In the beginning there will have been ruin.

Nothing can be determined out of context but every context is in a state of ruin.

Only fragment.

Consider the following, which serves as epigraph to David Wood's Introduction to the book *Derrida and Différance*: 'It is to Heraclitus that I refer myself in the last analysis'.[5] Like other instances of that strange and little-discussed genre of 'the epigraph', this particular epigraph is aphoristic in at least three ways: it is attributed (linked to a proper name, normally that of another author); it is separated off from what precedes and succeeds it and poses in some sense as 'sufficient unto itself'; and it is presented as a thought-provoking, even peremptory kind of truth-statement. This particular statement is attributed to Derrida but, as is often the case with epigraphs, its provenance is not specified. Epigraph in ruins then, as ruin.

'It is to Heraclitus that I refer myself in the last analysis': what is teleological and totalising in this reference to a reference to a 'last analysis' is always already in ruins. Let us try to enter into the swim of this by way of one of the most legendary of those aphoristic statements attributed to Heraclitus: 'One cannot step twice into the same river, nor can one grasp any mortal substance in a stable condition, but it scatters and again gathers; it forms and dissolves, and approaches and departs'.[6] Reading this after Derrida, as it were, it seems appropriate to suggest that one cannot step *once* into the same river — at least in so far as what enables us to think 'the same' is also that which divides it, makes it different from itself. Différance or the trace: that which cannot be traced back, 'in the last analysis', to any presence. This Heraclitean fragment evokes the uncanny, impossible 'origins' of western philosophy. It evokes ceaselessly, for example right now, the ghostliness of the present, of all arrivals and departures, of what is constantly unstable, *in destabilisation*. There is no simple 'step', for each step is out of step, made possible only by différance, by the footwork and waterworks of traces, and traces of traces. This différance, these traces, are themselves nowhere simply present (or simply absent): they do not coincide with themselves. Heraclitean–Derridean aphorism prompts us to think, 'in the last analysis', of ruins in ruin: there are only ruins (of the present, of perception, of experience) but these ruins are 'in themselves' in ruins, and so on, ceaselessly.

What is deconstruction? As if with this 'last analysis' of Heraclitus in mind, Derrida writes, in the Afterword to *Limited Inc*: 'before becoming a discourse, an organized practice that *resembles* a philosophy, a theory, a method, which it *is not*, in regard to those unstable stabilities or this destabilization that it makes its principal theme, "deconstruction" is firstly this destabilization on the move in, if one could speak thus, "the things themselves" ' (ATED, 147). As a transformative strategy without finality, as the destabilising differantial effects always already at work everywhere, deconstruction is never single but necessarily multiple and incomplete. Deconstruction is always already in ruins. There are only ever the ruins of deconstruction, and the deconstruction of ruins.

A few words about love or on the way towards love — among the ruins of philosophy. In 'Force of Law: The "Mystical Foundation of Authority" ', in the context of a discussion of Walter Benjamin, we may read the following:

> I do not see ruin as a negative thing. First of all, it is clearly not a thing. And then I would love to write, maybe with or following Benjamin, maybe against Benjamin [*after* Benjamin, in other words — N.R.], a short treatise on love of ruins. What else is there to love, anyway? One cannot love a monument, a work of architecture, an institution as such except in an experience itself precarious in its fragility: it hasn't always been there, it will not always be there, it is finite. And for this very reason I love it as mortal, through its birth and its death, through the ghost or the silhouette of its ruin, of my own — which it already is or prefigures. How can we love except in this finitude? Where else

would the right to love, indeed the love of right, come from? (FL, 1009)

Perhaps it will not be possible to know whether Derrida has written, or even could write, his 'short treatise on love of ruins'. Alternatively, we could suggest that he has never written anything else — nothing besides an extended, interruptive series of treatises on love of ruins.

Ostensibly, however, the most obvious example of such a treatise would be *Memoirs of the Blind: The Self-Portrait and Other Ruins*, first published in French in 1990. Here Derrida writes:

> The ruin is not in front of us; it is neither a spectacle nor a love object. It is experience itself: neither the abandoned yet still monumental fragment of a totality, nor, as Benjamin thought, simply a theme of baroque culture. It is precisely not a theme, for it ruins the theme, the position, the presentation or representation of anything and everything. (*MB*, 69)

Derrida is concerned to demonstrate — by way of a discourse (in the form of an exhibition catalogue) on various drawings of blind people and various self-portraits, mostly in the Louvre — that 'In the beginning, at the origin, there was ruin. At the origin comes ruin, ruin comes to the origin, it is what first comes and happens to the origin, in the beginning. With no promise of restoration' (*MB*, 65).

We could try to illustrate some of this, in other words some of the truth in drawing and the truth in painting, by considering the work of an artist to whom Derrida does not refer in his study, the Finnish painter Helene Schjerfbeck. More uncannily perhaps than any other self-portraits in twentieth-century painting, Schjerfbeck's appear to testify to Derrida's general 'hypothec', in *Memoirs of the Blind*, that 'A work is at once order and its ruin' (*MB*, 122). Schjerfbeck's self-portraits are ghostly, stunning, even terrifying.[7] They present us with a sense of what Derrida describes as 'the "Medusa" effect', whereby 'one cannot look in the face without coming face to face with a petrified objectivity, with death or blindness' (*MB*, 73). By the same deathly gesture, we encounter in these por-

Helene Schjerfbeck, 'Self-portrait, 1915';
pencil, watercolour, charcoal and silver leaf

By permission of the Turku Art Museum
Photo: Kari Lehtinen

Helene Schjerfbeck, 'Last self-portrait, 1945';
charcoal drawing on paper; Gyllenberg Collection, Helsinki

By permission of the Finnish National Gallery
Photo: The Central Art Archives/Hannu Aaltonen

traits the sense of a spectral force that divides narcissism from itself. If some of these Schjerfbeck self-portraits look imperious, they are so only as ghosts: these pictures address an impossibility of the gaze, both that of the self-portraitist herself and of our own.[8]

With its apocalyptic title and almost skeletonising minimalism, Schjerfbeck's 'Last Self-Portrait' (1945),[9] for example, at once seems to mirror, shatter and eclipse Derrida's proposition that 'The ruin does not supervene like an accident upon a monument that was intact only yesterday. In the beginning there is ruin. Ruin is that which happens to the image from the moment of the first gaze. Ruin is the self-portrait, this face looked at in the face as the memory of itself, what *remains* or *returns* as a specter from the moment one first looks at oneself and a figuration is eclipsed' (*MB*, 68).

Every self-portrait is a 'last self-portrait'.

Memoirs of the Blind sketches a magnificent kind of spectro-grammatology for thinking about the self-portrait. If every self-portrait is undecidably the self-portrait of a self-portrait, the figure or face of a Schjerfbeck self-portrait 'should be looking at us looking at [her] according to the law of an impossible and blinding reflexivity' (*MB*, 62). Like the self-portrait drawings of/by Henri Fantin-Latour about which Derrida speaks in *Memoirs of the Blind*, the self-portrait paintings of/by Helene Schjerfbeck call on us, call on our eyes, to bear witness to what makes a self-portrait at once possible and impossible. For, as Derrida puts it, 'the status of the self-portrait of the self-portraitist will always retain a hypothetical character. It always depends on the juridical effect of the title, on this verbal event that does not belong to the inside of the work but only to its parergonal border' (*MB*, 64). He then pushes this a bit further: 'If what is called a self-portrait depends on the fact that it is called "self-portrait", an act of naming should allow or *entitle* me to call just about anything a self-portrait, not only any drawing [or painting] ("portrait" or not) but anything that happens to me, anything by which I can be affected or let myself be affected' (*MB*, 65).

An aphorism, this aphorism, is a self-portrait.

'It only happens to me' (*JD ii*, 305), as Derrida asserts in 'Circumfession'; but what allows what only happens to me, this singularity of experience which would be the singularity of a self-portrait in the sense just outlined, is at the same time that which dissociates the self-portrait from itself, a parergonal act of naming which both belongs and does not belong to the self-portrait.

This is in part why, to adopt Derrida's phrase (*MB*, 65), one paints or writes like nobody — and like nobody else. 'I'm Nobody! Who are you?' as Emily Dickinson declares, in her almost inimitable fashion: aphoristically.[10]

Every poem is, in Dickinson's words, a 'letter to the World', a love letter or postcard of sorts:[11] a cryptic self-portrait or, as Derrida puts it, 'an open letter in which the secret appears, but indecipherably'.[12]

The 'Envois' in *The Post Card* (E, 3–256) constitute perhaps Derrida's most provocative 'self-portrait' and most obvious affront to the conventional requirements and expectations of philosophical discourse. This is philosophy in fragments, on postcards.

With the self-portrait, ruins and love in mind, let us take a detour via a volcano. Rather than propose an explicit reading of *Derrida's* postcard/s, let us try to read another, namely Wallace Stevens's 'A Postcard from the Volcano' (1936):

> Children picking up our bones
> Will never know that these were once
> As quick as foxes on the hill;
>
> And that in autumn, when the grapes
> Made sharp air sharper by their smell
> These had a being, breathing frost;
>
> And least will guess that with our bones
> We left much more, left what still is
> The look of things, left what we felt
>
> At what we saw. The spring clouds blow
> Above the shuttered mansion-house,
> Beyond our gate and the windy sky

> Cries out a literate despair.
> We knew for long the mansion's look
> And what we said of it became
>
> A part of what it is ... Children,
> Still weaving budded aureoles,
> Will speak our speech and never know,
>
> Will say of the mansion that it seems
> As if he that lived there left behind
> A spirit storming in blank walls,
>
> A dirty house in a gutted world,
> A tatter of shadows peaked to white,
> Smeared with the gold of the opulent sun.[13]

This postcard is about ruins, about transience and what remains of us after we die. This concern is inscribed in the figure of the mansion-house: this 'mansion' is inhabited, etymologically and otherwise, by a sense of the Latin *manere*, 'to remain', 'to stay'. Stevens's poem would seem to constitute a response to Wordsworth's question, in Book 5 of *The Prelude* (1805):

> Oh, why hath not the mind
> Some element to stamp her image on
> In nature somewhat nearer to her own?
> Why, gifted with such powers to send abroad
> Her spirit, must it lodge in shrines so frail?[14]

Why must the powers of human expression be constrained and confined by something as transient and insubstantial as the written or printed word? Stevens's poem is also about a 'spirit' – 'A spirit storming in blank walls' — and about the frailty of 'shrines', in other words the frailty of writing or books. The frail shrine in this case is a postcard. More particularly, however, Stevens's poem implies — in some respects apparently *against* Wordsworth — that the mind does have 'Some element to stamp her image on', that the mind can in some sense stamp a postcard, that there is the stamping and sending abroad of a postcard, that 'nature' in fact might itself be described as a postcard-effect. All of these things would be true, it may be added, even though this postcard does not reach its destination, indeed cannot be read, remains still to be read.

We have been sent a postcard from a hot place, a volcano, and we will never be through with reading it, or with being read by it. In fact we will never know whether we have even received it, or rather perhaps whether it has received *us*.

When we love we love till death.

'A Postcard from the Volcano' is a love-poem of a strikingly posthumous character. It is prosopopoeia in the strong sense — a postcard from the dead. Like Samuel Beckett's last published work, 'what is the word', Wallace Stevens's poem is intimately preoccupied with the sensuous and phenomenal, with what Beckett calls 'this this' — 'seeing all this . . . this this here'.[15] 'A Postcard from the Volcano' is about 'this this' — about 'these' bones, the 'sharp air' of autumn, 'the look of things'. It is about what we touch, smell, feel, hear and see. It is about the quickness of 'being' ('As quick as foxes on the hill') — both the quickness of being alive and the speed, brevity, transience of life. Stevens's postcard is an affirmative proclamation concerning our remains and ruins: it states that after our deaths we will have left behind not only 'our bones' but 'left much more, left what still is / The look of things, left what we felt / At what we saw'. The poem, in other words, proposes a logic of survival, a sense in which future generations (the 'children' of this poem) will be affected, inhabited, inscribed by our feelings and our speech. It is not simply a matter of what is transmitted from one generation to the next in genetic, psychological or ideological terms. Rather, 'A Postcard from the Volcano' presents the 'storming' affirmation of a radical unconscious or *nessence*, a ruinous sense of what is not known, of what one 'will never know'. This unconscious cannot be straightforwardly 'enshrined' (to adopt Wordsworth's sacralising term) even if it does have to do with fiction, with a certain literariness.

What can never be known — this peculiar and ruinous 'unconscious' — incorporates the reader, you and me. It draws any reading of this postcard into being a part of itself, 'a part of what it is'. What is enigmatic but ineluctable here is that we

are at once identified with the 'we' of the poem and with
the 'children'. Like the children in the poem who pick up the
bones of the dead, we pick up this postcard from the dead.
In so far as we are figured as both the 'we' of the poem and
the 'children', it would seem that there is no such thing as
'our speech', our own speech, our own perceptions and feelings. As 'children', the 'we' of the poem (and 'we' its readers)
are in turn ruinously affected, inhabited, inscribed by what
we will 'never know'. The postcard logic of this nessence is a
work of survival which traverses *us*, traverses every speaker,
every writer or reader. This inscription and traversal cannot
be assimilated to a logic of linear, transgenerational links
between unitary subjects: rather it is figured as a kind of
haunting and apocalyptic fictionality.

This emerges from the closing words of the postcard, in which
we read that these children 'will speak our speech and never
know', but *still* they 'Will say of the mansion that it seems . . .'.
The children will speak without knowing; they will speak what
they will never know. The last six lines evoke the apocalyptic
drama of 'A spirit storming in blank walls, / A dirty house in a
gutted world'. They present us with a phantasmagoric, fictive
'speech' — a speech which is nevertheless never known. In
so far as the final six lines of the poem give us a figure of the
poet ('he that lived there') or of the poetic or volcanic 'spirit',
this figure is always already in tatters. More than this, the
very figuration of this ruined figure is in ruins. This final scene
of destruction and disappearance offers us the very figure of
a poem, as defined by Derrida in 'Che cos'è la poesia?':

> a mark addressed to you, left and confided with you, is
> accompanied by an injunction, in truth it is instituted in this
> very order which, in its turn, constitutes you, assigning your
> origin or giving rise to you: destroy me, or rather render my
> support invisible to the outside, in the world (this is already the
> trait of all dissociations, the history of transcendences), in any
> case do what must be done so that the provenance of the mark
> remains from now on unlocatable and unrecognizable. (Che, 227)

The aphorism is poetic. It says: *destroy me*.

Yet Stevens's postcard not only offers us a figure or picture of the poetic or 'poematic' (Che, 233), in Derrida's terms, but — in its evocation of unknowing readers (the 'children') and unknown addressees (you, for instance) — it also explicitly narrates or allegorises this 'destroy me', this unrecognisability *within itself*. Like Derrida's *Post Card*, in fact.

Stevens has much to say about 'the relations between poetry and painting', for example in his essay of that title.[16] He draws an analogy with Picasso's aphoristic proposal that a painting is a horde of destructions by suggesting that 'a poem is a horde of destructions'.[17] He also remarks on the correspondence whereby 'Poetry and painting alike create through composition'.[18] Such characterisations will perhaps indicate the intimacy which Stevens regarded poetry and painting as sharing and the extent to which this intimacy entailed a combination of the compositional and the decompositional or 'decreative'.[19] If the picture on/of this postcard is a self-portrait — and it is tempting to read into the painterly language of the final lines not only the 'blank' of a canvas but perhaps also the 'shadows' of the most improbable signature (the 'w.s.' of what is 'white' and at the same time 'smeared', like paint, but also like a name) — this is not just a self-portrait of ruins, but the ghostly ruins of the effacement of the ghostly ruins of every self-portrait.[20] It is the opulence of the impossible.

'A poem', says Derrida, 'I never sign(s) it' (Che 237).

It is speech, in ruins. Prosopopoeia — a voice from the dead — is here doubled: this posthumous postcard ends with the uncanny evocation of a phantomatic 'tatter', a 'peaked' volcanic 'spirit' which has itself been created, woven, budded or brought forth within a speech that its speakers will 'never know'. What most forcefully remains here is what is most fictive and impossible, a 'spirit' which is 'left behind', yet gone without trace, beyond knowledge. The ruined figure, the figure of ruin brought forth in the last six lines of this poem has no place to be — except in this unconscious speech, this fiction and phantasmagoria of 'blank walls' and 'a gutted world, / ... / Smeared with the gold of the opulent sun' — yet at the same time these lines fold in, double back, haunt what has gone before, in such a way as to imply that this doubling and haunting has constitutive force. There is no speech which is not inscribed by the posthumous. This irrevocably duplicitous, chiasmatic posthumous speech is not the voicing of something that is negative. Rather it is affirmative, unceasing, *still* happening — like the children 'Still weaving budded aureoles'.²¹

In his essay 'On Transience' (1916), Freud writes:

> A time may indeed come when the pictures and statues which we admire to-day will crumble to dust, or a race of men may follow us who no longer understand the works of our poets and thinkers, or a geological epoch may even arrive when all animate life upon the earth ceases; but since the value of all this beauty and perfection is only determined by its significance for our own emotional lives, it has no need to survive us and is therefore independent of absolute duration. (*PFL*, 14: 288)

Freud goes on to assert that all of this is 'incontestable' (288). But isn't it contestable in a number of respects, and not only from the late twentieth-century ecological and political perspective of living on a planet the beauties and very existence of which are imperilled in ways that Freud was simply unable to foresee? Times have moved on since 'On Transience'. Above all, this passage from 'On Transience' presents a classic instance of what might be called the Freudian egotistical sublime: the transience of 'all this beauty and perfection' need be conceived and theorised only in terms of 'our own emotional lives' and (as Freud's essay goes on to suggest) in terms of our own 'mourning' for its anticipated loss. It is in this essay too, we may recall, that Freud makes the remarkable corollary claim that 'Mourning . . . however painful it may be, comes to a spontaneous end' (*PFL* 14: 290). It is not simply a question of criticising Freud's conception of mourning to the extent that it is, as Kathleen Woodward for example has pointed out, rigidly teleological, that it involves what she describes as 'a peculiar kind of piety, an almost ethical injunction to kill the dead and to adjust ourselves to "reality" '.²² It is rather the question of a different kind of injunction and a different kind of ethics — one that might accord with Derrida's notion of *demi-deuil*, a half-mourning irreducible to the Freudian opposition of introjection ('normal' mourning) or incorporation (so-called abnormal or refused mourning).[23] It is a matter of an exhumation of the very grounds of mourning, especially in so far as mourning is construed as 'merely' supplementary to the identity and experience of the subject. 'A Postcard from the Volcano' erupts, disrupts, burns up every notion of mourning that would be formulated on the basis of a self-identical subject.

Stevens's postcard suggests that there is no perception, no feeling, no speech or writing which is not phantomised, brought forth by a kind of radically fictional, poetic nessence. Reading is doubled, haunted, inscribed by postcard-effects of what we will 'never know'. We can never be at one with ourselves, with our speech or our feelings. 'A Postcard from the Volcano' suggests a theory of reading (and, by the same token it may be said, a love of reading) opposed to the very equation of identity-as-authority, at odds with everything in our culture which upholds the identity and authority of the self and the identity and authority of its speech.[24]

In *Memoirs of the Blind*, Derrida observes of 'the love of ruins': 'A narcissistic melancholy, a memory — in mourning — of love itself. How to love anything other than the possibility of ruin? Than an impossible totality? Love is as old as this ageless ruin — at once originary, an infant even, and already old' (68–9). Mourning is the very condition of love, 'love itself'. Let us recall what Derrida says in 'Aphorism Countertime' — that 'I love because the other is the other, because its time will never be mine' (AC, 420), and that whenever I love 'a law *engages* me to the death of the other' (AC, 422). This is also to acknowledge that love is ghostly; it is traced by what is radically other (by death, in short), even in the experience of the most 'ecstatic communion' (AC, 421), the most intense rapport.

A fragmentary anecdote to conclude. There was an ICA seminar in London in 1985, involving a discussion between Jacques Derrida and Geoff Bennington, subsequently published as 'On Colleges and Philosophy' (OCP). At the end of the discussion there were questions from the so-called 'floor', including one from Jacqueline Rose who preceded her question (which was about the relationship between Derrida's and Lacan's work) by saying to Derrida: 'I was amused by your saying that "everything lives", "everybody who is living, lives through deconstruction" at the end of your paper, because about two years ago Julia Kristeva, sitting in exactly that place [in an earlier seminar at the ICA], ended her talk by saying that everything that lives, lives through love and psychoanalysis' (OCP, 226). Then Rose went on to put her question. By way of response — and this does not appear in the published transcript of the occasion and consequently it marks the beginning of the anecdote (as well as the necessary ruination or impossibility of the anecdote in general, to the extent that an anecdote, as 'secret, private or hitherto unpublished narrative(s) or details of history' (OED), as what is not given out (ἀν + ἐκ–διδόναι), can come into existence only by ceasing to be itself, by ceasing to be strictly anecdotal) — Derrida stood up and pointed reverentially at his chair exclaiming, with seeming incredulity, 'Julia Kristeva? Sat here? In exactly this place?' Derrida's subsequent remarks included a sort of repetition and differentiation of the formulation Rose had recalled from Kristeva: specifically, he observed that 'deconstruction is love'. This statement does not appear in the published transcript either; but in December 1991 I wrote and asked him about this statement, 'deconstruction is love': would it be fair of me to quote him on something unpublished? Or would he wish to forget the remark? In his letter in response (13 December 1991), Derrida 'authorises' me 'de grand coeur' to cite this unpublished phrase. ('Mais bien entendu, si vous voulez bien en prendre la responsabilité, je vous autorise de grand coeur à citer cette phrase non publiée ["Deconstruction is love"]'.) I say 'authorise' rather than 'permit' (as a translation of 'je vous autorise . . .') in order to highlight a certain force of laughter, telepathic laughter, the call and the ruins of a laughter beyond being.

Deconstruction is love. That would be the final aphorism here, but only on condition that it could never be mine — or Jacques Derrida's either.

Notes

1 Rodolphe Gasché, *The Tain of the Mirror: Derrida and the Philosophy of Reflection* (Cambridge, Mass.: Harvard University Press, 1986).

2 The present chapter is more generally concerned with the 'poetic' in relation to Derrida's work: the 'dramatic' is more specifically a focus in Chapter 7.

3 See Maurice Blanchot, 'The Athenaeum', trans. Deborah Esch and Ian Balfour, *Studies in Romanticism*, 22 (1983): 163–72, and Philippe Lacoue-Labarthe and Jean-Luc Nancy, *The Literary Absolute: The Theory of Literature in German Romanticism*, trans. Philip Barnard and Cheryl Lester (Albany: State University of New York Press, 1988).

4 'The absolute aphorism: a proper name' (AC, 433), as the final aphoristic section of 'Aphorism Countertime' has it.

5 Jacques Derrida, epigraph to David Wood's Introduction to *Derrida and Différance*, eds Robert Bernasconi and David Wood (Evanston, Illinois: Northwestern University Press, 1988), ix.

6 *The Art and Thought of Heraclitus: An Edition of the Fragments with Translation and Commentary*, by Charles H. Kahn (Cambridge: Cambridge University Press, 1979), 53.

7 For what is perhaps the best collection published to date of reproductions of Schjerfbeck's pictures, see *Helene Schjerfbeck* (Helsinki: The Finnish National Gallery Ateneum, 1992). This is the catalogue for the superb exhibition which was staged at the Ateneum, in Helsinki, from 2 February to 5 April 1992.

8 In at least one of the 'last' self-portraits (*Helene Schjerfbeck*, no.502), this impossibility is specifically invoked through its titling: 'Self-Portrait with Closed Eyes'. But see, too, nos 500 and 501.

9 See *Helene Schjerfbeck*, no.506.

10 Emily Dickinson, *Complete Poems*, ed. Thomas H. Johnson (London: Faber and Faber, 1970), 133.

11 Emily Dickinson, *Complete Poems*, 211.

12 See the back cover of *The Post Card*: 'You were reading a somewhat retro loveletter, the last in history. But you have not yet received it. Yes, its lack or excess of address prepares it to fall into all hands: a post card, an open letter in which the secret appears, but indecipherably.'

13 *The Collected Poems of Wallace Stevens* (New York: Alfred Knopf, 1978), 158–9.

14 William Wordsworth, *The Prelude 1799, 1805, 1850*, eds Jonathan

Wordsworth, M. H. Abrams and Stephen Gill (New York: Norton, 1979), Book V, 44–8.

15 See Samuel Beckett, 'what is the word', in *As the Story Was Told: Uncollected and Late Prose* (London: John Calder, 1990), 131–4.

16 Wallace Stevens, 'The Relations between Poetry and Painting', in *The Necessary Angel: Essays on Reality and the Imagination* (New York: Vintage Books, n.d.), 159–76.

17 *The Necessary Angel*, 161.

18 *The Necessary Angel*, 163.

19 On 'decreation' (a term Stevens takes from Simone Weil), see *The Necessary Angel*, 174–5.

20 Cf. Geoffrey Bennington's account of another deconstructive 'spirit', in 'Spirit's Spirit Spirits Spirit', in his *Legislations: The Politics of Deconstruction* (London and New York: Verso, 1994), 196–206.

21 The various kinds of doubling of 'we' and the 'children' are evoked in the very figure of an aureole, as a halo or ring of light surrounding a figure, doubling its outline. The most apposite form of the aureole in this context would perhaps be the *vesica piscis*, 'a halo in the form of two circular arcs each (properly) passing through the other's centre, enclosing the whole figure' (*Chambers*).

22 Kathleen Woodward, *Aging and Its Discontents: Freud and Other Fictions* (Bloomington: Indiana University Press, 1991), 116. Woodward's study explores the opposition between being 'old' and being 'young'. She seeks to question and disturb among other things the privileging of 'youth' that is a theoretical basis of Freud's thought and consequently of psychoanalysis in general. In the context of Stevens's 'Postcard', it may be ventured that, to the extent that the poem works with an opposition of being young (being 'children') and being old (being those who 'knew for long the mansion's look', being associated with what is 'peaked' or in tatters), it also reverses, doubles, splits and dissolves this opposition. Unconscious parents, these children bring us forth, they 'speak our speech', they are our precursors, our creators. The children are at once the future and they are ourselves, they *are* 'we'.

23 On *demi-deuil*, half- or part-mourning, see for example *JD i*, 146–8.

24 For a fuller discussion of these issues, see Leo Bersani, *The Culture of Redemption* (Cambridge, Mass.: Harvard University Press, 1990).

7

Foreign Body: 'The deconstruction of a pedagogical institution and all that it implies'

> Thought is an infection.
>
> Wallace Stevens
>
> The virus is ageless.
>
> *JD ii*, 92

— What did you say?

(*The audience looks and listens.*)

— There is a foreign body in our midst.

— Why do you say that?

— I'm not really sure. 'Sometimes I feel it coming all the same. Then I go all queer.'

— That's Vladimir, in Beckett's *Waiting for Godot*.[1]

— Suppose stage directions take on a voice, the voice of a foreign body, 'old style' omniscience, 'new style' telepathy: Then I go all queer. (*He takes off his hat, peers inside it, feels about inside it, shakes it, puts it on again.*) How shall I say? Relieved and at the same time . . .

— (*He searches for the word*) . . .

— appalled.

— (*With emphasis.*)

— AP-PALLED.

— (*He takes off his hat again, peers inside it.*)

— Funny.

— (*He knocks on the crown as if to dislodge a foreign body, peers into it again, puts it on again.*)

— Nothing to be done.

— There is a foreign body in our midst. In saying this, I admit to not really knowing what I mean, to not really knowing what *we* might mean, if we were to say, in some collective fashion (to be determined): There is a foreign body in our midst.

— It's beginning to sound like a quotation.

— Perhaps it was a quotation from the start. 'There is a foreign body in our midst': with these words was announced the setting up or institution of a new research seminar at the University of Stirling, in Scotland, in February 1993. The posters, which were put up around the university, bore only those words, together with an open invitation to the first meeting, at a specified time and place, the following week.

— But what will have been the identity of a foreign body?

— What is it to say, here in the university, in a form that is not only constative or descriptive but also perhaps performative, 'There is a foreign body in our midst'?

— Everything that follows will circle around these questions, which are questions about the supposedly pure, uncontaminated nature of a 'serious' speech act, about the relationship between performatives and institutions, about the forms of mutual dependence and contamination at work in the paradoxy of the phrase 'the identity of a foreign body'. In short, what is going on in the idea of an institution — and most specifically a research seminar within the university, a research group or research body — calling itself Foreign Body?

— The focus for this presentation

— if it is one –

— is the work of Jacques Derrida. His writings might, provisionally at least, be described as one of the primary 'influences' behind Foreign Body. Derrida's work, his thinking, is infectious. Like what Freud famously called the 'plague' (his dysphemism for 'psychoanalysis' in an aside to Jung as the ship carried them into New York Harbor in 1909), deconstruction has been widely figured as an infection. Deconstruction began to spread through Anglophone universities in the late 1970s: one doesn't really hear talk of, say, new historicism *spreading* in this sense. This was followed by the so-called domestication of deconstruction, of which it may for the moment simply be remarked that, if deconstruction is (as I hope to make clear) a kind of parasite or parasitism, then the project of domesticating it is a more itchingly paradoxical matter than may have been supposed.[2] In the present paper, then, Derrida's work functions as a kind of foreign body.

— That's interesting. It's putting various ideas into my

head for other ways of trying to think about 'influence' and that strange event called 'reading': tradition as virus; infection and intertextuality; reading as allergic reaction; the author as always already inhabited by the foreign bodies of others; the body of every text as always already parasited . . .

— Yes, indeed, for it's also a question of recognising how Derrida's work in turn functions as a kind of foreign body, in relation to other writings. Derrida's texts are profoundly parasitical upon other texts, not only seeking to inhabit their space but also to suggest that 'their' space was always already infected by the force and effects of what his reading of them introduces. A kind of philosophical telepathy, perhaps . . .

— I'm a bit concerned about the emphasis you're putting on Derrida's work. Isn't there a danger of fetishising, even sacralising the name of Derrida? Is the import of his work basically synonymous with what Foreign Body is about?

— The danger you speak of is no doubt there. This is always the case when you invoke a particular author in affirmative terms and present his or her work as exemplary. But there are also questions of strategy involved. On the one hand I would argue that Foreign Body could be described without any specific reference to Derrida at all. I could present it, for example, by focusing on another body of texts (Plato's, or Nietzsche's, or Elizabeth Bowen's) or by focusing on different forms or media altogether, such as the paintings of Steven Campbell, the music of Talking Heads, the television and film-making of David Lynch. But from a strategic perspective it is perhaps worth acknowledging that Derrida's writings provide, after all, an overt and prolonged meditation on the notion of the foreign body and that they do so in ways which are, I believe, particularly susceptible to a concise rendering or recital.

— And on the other hand?

— On the other hand, let's also not forget that what's going on here is after all a deconstruction of the figure of the author, of the coherence of the body of a work, of the relation between a so-called primary text and its exposition or translation, a deconstruction of the notions of tradition and influence, even of language itself.

— Language itself? My word!

— Whose? Did someone speak?

— I'm not sure whose words these are I'm speaking. Can you help me?

— What words are you referring to?

— Foreign Body.

— All of Derrida's work — the entire oeuvre (including, it may be ventured, what is still to come, not yet published or even not yet written) — can be encapsulated within the words 'foreign body', to the extent that these are words at all quite, or that we know what we mean when we call them 'words'. As he puts it in his Foreword to Nicolas Abraham and Maria Torok's *The Wolf Man's Magic Word*: 'A certain foreign body is here working over our household words' (F, xxv). Whether it is under the rubric of contamination or impurity, parasitism or 'double chiasmatic invagination' (LG, 238), the crypt or the re-mark,[3] all of Derrida's work can be read in terms of the notion of foreign body. Participating in a chain of non-synonymic substitutions that would include différance, the trace, iterability, the re-mark, the hymen, pharmakon, signature, telepathy, ruins and so on, 'foreign body' would name that which makes every identity, all language, perception and experience different from itself. This may help clarify the still prevalent misconception of Derrida's work as constituting a kind of linguisticism (the misreading and misrepresentation, for example, of his aphoristic proposition that 'there is nothing outside the text', the mistaken belief that this means that everything is in books, all experience is linguistic, and so forth). Rather I would suggest that the opposite is the case: there is a certain foreign body which works *over* our language, over what we say and read and write, and which corresponds perhaps more closely to a notion of what Derrida refers to as 'the "other of language" ', the other 'which is beyond language and which summons language' (DO, 123), or what he talks about as 'force' when he proposes that 'Force is the other of language without which language would not be what it is' (FS, 27). The foreign body, like the trace, would also demand to be thought in relation to the ahuman or inhuman — that is to say, in relation to Derrida's contention that there is nothing essentially human about language and consequently that 'man is not the only political animal' (ATED, 136) — with all the implications that that carries with it.

— Carrying implications. Like carrying foreign bodies?

— In a sense, yes. You cannot get away from this logic of the foreign body. Ask Howard Hughes.

— Howard who?

— But to demonstrate, as Derrida does for example in 'Signature Event Context' and 'Limited Inc', that a logic of parasitism affects the distinctions in speech act theory between 'serious' and 'non-serious', 'standard' and 'non-standard', 'normal' and 'abnormal', 'citation' and 'non-citation', 'literal' and 'metaphorical' (cf. LI, 34), is *also* to engage with a deconstruction of the distinctions between parasitism and non-parasitism themselves. Elsewhere — and here I quote a so-called Derrida 'bootleg', a text which figures as a kind of foreign body in relation to the laws of authorship and publishing — Derrida speaks of 'the terrible monotony' of what he says and teaches, and in particular of the degree to which all of his work constitutes 'a sort of theory of the parasite, parasitology' (TPB, 18); but to respond to this terrible monotony and to reckon with such a parasitology is before anything else to encounter the paradoxy of the parasite *as a foreign body*. As Derrida puts it in 'Limited Inc': 'the parasite is by definition never simply *external*, never simply something that can be excluded from or kept outside of the body "proper", shut out from the "familial" table or house' (LI, 90). As foreign body, the parasite both belongs and does not belong to what it inhabits: breaching and compromising the identity of the body or host which it inhabits, its 'own' identity is of a différant order, being at once *para-* ('beside') and *non-para-*, inside and outside, coming to figure what is at once the same as and different from itself.

— In the same passage of 'Limited Inc' from which you have just cited (or parasited), Derrida writes:

> The parasite then 'takes place'. And at bottom, whatever violently 'takes place' or occupies a site is always *something* of a parasite. *Never quite* taking place is thus part of its performance, of its success as an event, of its taking-place. (LI, 90)

Parasitism might then be understood as a kind of synonym

for iterability — for what *enables* the 'standard' case of promises or other so-called performative statements and their
'normal' effects but which at the same time means that such
statements are, 'from [their] very inception on, parasited,
harboring and haunted by the possibility of being repeated
in *all kinds of ways*, of which the theater, poetry, or soliloquy
are only examples' (LI, 90). But parasitism can be linked with
iterability only on condition of recognising that it is not identical with itself; parasitism is parasited or, as Derrida puts it in
that bootleg you were referring to, 'the *meaning* of parasite
parasites itself' (TPB, 18). Here I am, going all queer again. I
feel it coming. Iterability or parasitism conform to a foreign-
body logic to the extent that they are not self-identical but
figure an implant of foreignness or otherness (*iter, itara*: see
SEC, 7) *within* the same. Is that right? Have I picked up your
meaning here?

   — Yes, though in a sense perhaps only to the extent that
this meaning could never be purely mine, or ours, or 'theirs',
for that matter. There is something parasitical in everything
that violently 'takes place' — and this would include, as I'll
try to suggest, not only the taking place, the putting into
place, the institution of a research seminar called 'Foreign
Body', but also the very institution of the university within
which it takes place — such 'taking place' is always in part
parasitical.

   — You promise to come back to that?

   — Yes, I promise. Every event, in its very singularity,
presupposes some contamination. As Derrida observes:

> What happens is always some *contamination*. The uniqueness of
> the event is this coming about of a singular relation between the
> unique and its repetition, its iterability. The event comes about,
> or promises itself initially, only by thus compromising itself by
> the singular contamination of the singular and what shares it. It
> comes about as impurity — and impurity here is chance. (TSICL,
> 68–9)

But inasmuch as another name for such contamination would
be 'chance', there can be no law or programme determining
the nature or degree of contamination. Rather there is what
he refers to in 'Limited Inc' as 'a law of undecidable contami-

nation' (LI, 59). Every so-called performative statement —
including the inaugural proposition that 'There is a foreign
body in our midst' — is at once haunted and structured by
its capacity for 'being repeated in *all kinds of ways*', as well
as by the necessary possibility that it may go astray, that it
may fail to be recognised or fail to perform itself. In this sense,
then, no performative statement ever quite takes place: '*never
quite* taking place is thus part of its performance, of its success
as an event, of its taking-place'. As a seminar, meeting regularly or intermittently, as a research group with its own idiom
(both singular and repeatable), Foreign Body never quite
takes place, and it is in the repeated singularity of never
quite taking place that Foreign Body generates its effects,
proliferates its concerns, takes its chances.

— I'm not sure I follow. What do you mean by a seminar
which never quite takes place? Does that apply to what is
happening right now, in this seminar here?

— Of course.

— It all sounds rather improbable to me.

— Yes, it is: Foreign Body is improbable. It is as improbable as a signature, as Derrida would say. The *improbable* is
what he defines as precisely 'having little chance of coming
to pass *and* in any case impossible to prove' (LI, 33).

— Where does that leave us?

— Us?

— There is a certain foreign body working over the words
'foreign body' and over the proposition that 'There is a foreign
body in our midst'. This proposition is haunted, and dis-
comforting perhaps, not only because of the ways in which it
is parasitical upon a certain kind of centrism, preying on the
thought of what is at the heart of us, in the very midst of us,
and because it by the same gesture throws up or swallows a
peculiar uncertainty as to what may be meant by 'our midst'
(in the midst of each of us, within ourselves, within the bodies
of each of us, here and now, in this room? Or in the midst of
us collectively, as a group, in the midst of this room? Or in
the midst of so-called humanity in general? Or of so-called
animality in general?), but also because it remains perhaps
undecidable whether the statement is describing *or* promising
something, whether it concerns the present ('There *is* a

foreign body') or the future (the foreign body is to-come: it comes from the future, 'I feel it coming'). If it is part of this promise that it *recalls* — for instance that its resonance in some measure depends on a parasitical association with the funereal statement that 'In the midst of life we are in death' — this recalling equally belongs to the future, but as a future that will never become present. 'Foreign body' could indeed be called (or recalled as) 'death', at least in so far as this name can be given (as it sometimes is in Derrida's work) for that otherness which haunts every mark, spoken or written, every perception and all experience.

— You mean something along the lines of Vladimir's evocation, 'Down in the hole, lingeringly, the grave-digger puts on the forceps'?[4]

— Yes, to evoke or evocate: 'to call up from the dead' (*Chambers*). But the foreign body of this 'death' is not negative: rather it is the condition of possibility of every identity, of the movement of 'life' as such and of every institution. Another name for this foreign body would be necessity, and above all the necessity of chance. It is for this reason that, in its own interruptive, unpredictable fashion, the seminar called Foreign Body aligns itself to Derrida's observation, in *Of Grammatology*, that 'The future can only be anticipated in the form of an absolute danger' (*OG*, 5). Foreign Body, then, is apocalyptic, vigilant, critical. It listens out for the *big bang* in the sense that that may, 'at the origin of the universe, have produced a noise which one can consider as still not having reached *us*' (T, 7). It traces the apocalypse of every alignment.

— This doesn't exactly sound like a bundle of laughs.

— Yes, yes. You're quite right. It's threatening and fraught with danger. But it *is also* a bundle of laughs.

— It's a bundle of voices.

— It says come.

— It tries to start out from the fact that (in Timothy Clark's words) 'Thinking and *risk* ought to be inseparable'.[5]

— It affirms the opening of the future itself, the telepathic coming of the big bang, the chimeras of incessant grafting.

— The seminar called Foreign Body has to do with grafting. If, as Derrida argues, nothing can be determined out of context but no context can itself be saturated, it would be true to say that there is always grafting: one context can always be grafted on to another, indeed the movement of grafting (like that of recontextualisation) is incessant, even if this grafting is never pure, indeed can never be pure. Thanks to the double pin-heads of a colon (and a colon itself, let us recall, introduces a kind of foreign body, coming from the Greek *kolon*, 'limb', 'member'), the title of this presentation grafts 'foreign body' to another phrase: 'The deconstruction of a pedagogical institution and all that it implies.' These words come from that bizarre parasitical footnote —

— Hang on, could I add a footnote to that? I mean, isn't it the case that every footnote is parasitical? Its imprint stamps the main body of the text as incomplete, in need of supplementation. A footnote disturbs, in the very equivocation of its name, the assurance of what constitutes the body of a text: is a footnote at the foot of the text, below and outside the text, or is it *part* of the body, a sort of internal foot? The footnote is at once supplementary to and part of the so-called main body of the text which thus becomes in turn disarticulated, dismembered, foreign to itself . . .

— Was that an oral footnote?

— Mum's the word.[6]

— that bizarre parasitical footnote (I was saying) called 'Border Lines', which spreads like an infection below that other text 'Living On'. Here Derrida writes:

> A politico-institutional problem of the University: it, like all teaching in its traditional form, and perhaps all teaching whatever, has as its ideal, with exhaustive translatability, the effacement of language [*la langue*]. The deconstruction of a pedagogical institution and all that it implies. What this institution cannot bear, is for anyone to tamper with [*toucher à*; also 'touch', 'change', 'concern oneself with'] language, meaning *both* the *national* language *and*, paradoxically, an ideal of translatability that neutralizes this national language. Nationalism and universalism. What this institution cannot bear is a transformation that leaves intact neither of these two complementary poles. It can bear more readily the most apparently revolutionary ideological sorts of 'content', if only that content does not touch the borders of language [*la langue*] and of all the juridico-political contracts that it guarantees. (BL, 93–5, tr. mod.)

Here and elsewhere in 'Border Lines' Derrida's concern is with translation as that which is at once necessary and impossible, and with a transformation of the theory and practice of translation as, precisely, transformation (cf. *P*, 20). The demand here is to reckon with the idea that, as he puts it later in this same parasitical text, 'One never writes either in one's own language or in a foreign language' (BL, 101).

— You can say that again.

— One never writes either in one's own language or in a foreign language. The logic of this double-bind is no doubt more troubling than, for example, Freud's well-known suggestion that 'We ourselves speak a language that is foreign' (*PFL*, 14: 341). For the foreignness in Freud's formulation is implicitly totalising — suggesting that we 'only' and always speak to ourselves and to each other in a foreign language. Derrida's proposition, on the other hand, upsets the very basis on which the foreign and non-foreign might be thought.

That translation is both necessary and impossible does not constitute some sort of abstract indeterminacy — a paradox to be momentarily wondered at and then accordingly dismissed. Rather the double-bind of this necessity and impossibility *affects* and *infects* all teaching in the most decisive ways. It is as part of what he tentatively refers to as a new enlightenment that Derrida argues that the logic of such a double-bind be acknowledged, analysed and elucidated. Disrupting the distinctions between nationalism and universalism, showing them to be foreign to themselves, bringing out the limits of the ideal of 'exhaustive translatability' through crossings or transgressions from a 'classical model of transportable univocality or of formalizable polysemia' over into 'dissemination' (BL, 93), Derrida's work is concerned with that which is both 'intolerable' (95) for institutions and yet, at the same time, always already *within* institutions.

'The deconstruction of a pedagogical institution and all that it implies': this sentence is, *stricto sensu*, not a sentence. In lacking a main verb and thus presenting a kind of deformation of grammar, an estrangement of the body of a grammatical sentence, this sentence has no time — and all the time in the world. The deconstruction of a pedagogical institution is not something that is happening now, in a self-identical present, nor is it something that will or might happen, in some future that could become present. What is implied by the deconstruction of a pedagogical institution is the always already, that movement of 'destabilization' or transformation already at work, on the move, in ' "things themselves" ' (ATED, 147), that is to say in the very grounding, setting forth or instituting of an institution. As Geoffrey Bennington has succinctly put it, 'Institutions in general are in deconstruction "before" deconstruction is in institutions' (*JD i*, 266). The word 'before', here, is in quotation marks, it may be noted, in order to indicate the disturbance and dislocation of temporality — the undecidable force of the 'always already' that is inscribed there. For the 'always already' of deconstruction belongs at once to a past that never existed and to what Derrida calls 'the opening of the future itself, a future which does not allow itself to be modalised or modified into the form of the present, which allows itself neither to be foreseen nor pro-grammed' (Aft, 200). The 'before' of deconstruction would then be encrypted here —

— Where?

— There is a foreign body in our midst.

— Grafting (itself on to) the deconstruction of a pedagogical institution, then, 'Foreign Body' is the name for a research seminar and a research group within a university — the University of Stirling or another university. Within the university, but in the form of, precisely, a foreign body. Belonging and not belonging to a pedagogical institution, concerned with what makes that institution both immensely valuable and impossible, Foreign Body has two interrelated or mutually parasitic concerns: (1) an attention to and exploration of forms of foreign body in so far as this concept may promise to be productive for the analysis of a range of discourses and practices, including literature, history, philosophy, film and mediology, psychology and psychoanalysis, politics and so on; and (2) a focus on the foreign body at an institutional level, that is to say analyses of institutions and institutionalisation as such, including an unceasing interrogation of Foreign Body as an institution, a strange or foreign institution in the sense that it is an institution-within-institution and thus perhaps the very model of every institution, the exemplification of every institution as quasi-institution, as foreign to itself.

— Doesn't this make Foreign Body rather an arcane and exclusive sort of thing?

— Quite the opposite. I'd say that Foreign Body is less exclusive than the university itself and that, far from being tucked away within its inner recesses, Foreign Body is in fact in some respects perhaps *larger*, more open and more democratic than the university of which it is apparently only a part. But if you'll just stop asking questions I will try to get on to explain this a bit more.

— But how does all this work out in practical terms? What about the relations between students and staff? How is the whole thing run?

— It's run on a model of multiple voices. It seeks to be, in principle, non-authoritarian, for example in the sense it seeks to put distinctions between teacher, postgraduate, undergraduate, analyst, analysand, member of the public or whatever, into suspension within the context of a Foreign Body meeting. At Stirling meetings usually take place in the evening, when the university is otherwise more or less deserted. Professional titles are dropped, there are no introductions. The person or persons presenting the seminar just start when and where they wish. The topic can, as I say, vary considerably: it may be about Heidegger and the force of reason in the university; the *Alien* movies; vampirism; the place of telephones in the work of Raymond Chandler; the ideological framing of Shakespeare; a Freud case-history; the concept of telepathy; hunting; the paintings of Seurat; somnambulistic passions.[7] In each instance the interest is, provisionally at least, in the articulation of a logic of the foreign body: of how particular institutions, media, texts, discourses and disciplines are inhabited, haunted, even constituted by what they cannot tolerate, by what they cannot acknowledge, by what is alien, external, contaminatory.

At a micro- and local level, Foreign Body could be said to affirm, transmit, translate in various respects the concerns of the International College of Philosophy, for example as Derrida outlines these in 'Sendoffs'. Continually constituting and reconstituting itself, setting up and disordering itself, Foreign

Body's concern is to work 'without assurance and without tranquillity' and 'never suture with the assurance of a body of knowledge, a doctrine or dogma' (Send, 12). Foreign Body is concerned with 'provoking new research' and 'making inaugural incursions' (13), including forms and 'ways of research whose *legitimacy* has not yet been recognised' (20). It is engaged with what Derrida refers to in 'The Principle of Reason' as 'new modes of questioning that are also a new relation to language and tradition, a new *affirmation*, and new ways of taking responsibility' (PR, 15). Such an affirmation responds, in short, to what can be called the current state of the university, at least in Britain and North America, that is to say this force of affirmation entails new ways of thinking about the institution of the university now that it has become clear that the university today is a 'ruined concept'.[8] No longer governed in any convincing or meaningful sense either by a principle of reason or by the idea of culture, the university is now, as Bill Readings recently suggested, 'headless'.[9] Guided only by the empty, even nihilistic so-called criteria of 'excellence' and 'quality', the contemporary university presents itself in such a fashion that, more clearly perhaps than ever before, its identity demands to be rethought.

The university is headless, it is a ghost.[10] And if a research group concerns itself with what Derrida calls 'possibilities that arise at the outer limits of the authority and the power of the principle of reason' (PR, 14) — that is to say, with kinds of work, kinds of thinking which necessarily confront and put into question the principle of reason (emerging out of women's studies, peace studies, deconstruction and psychoanalysis, for instance), and if this research seminar establishes itself as a kind of interrogation centre for the interrogation *of* the centre, the interrogation of every centrism (logo-, phallogo-, ethno-, anthrocentrism), including the interrogation of the model of interrogation as such, this seminar itself would necessarily be haunted — positively, affirmatively. Having no simple way of being accommodated, appropriated or assimilated, Foreign Body would never quite take place. That which announces, declares or promises the coming into being of the seminar — 'There is a foreign body in our midst' — is itself haunted, like the university, in its very inception, in the very moment of its institutionalisation. As Derrida puts it, in the essay 'Mochlos; or, The Conflict of the Faculties', 'the foundation of a university institution is not a university event' (Mo, 30). To declare and name the institution of a university or of a research seminar within that university is to institute by declaring and by naming — for instance with the words 'There is a foreign body in our midst' or (which would have been in effect the same thing) 'We hereby propose to set up (and therefore do set up) a research seminar called Foreign Body'. Such a declaration conforms to the structure and logic of the American Declaration of Independence analysed by Derrida: 'One cannot decide — and that's the interesting thing, the force and the coup of force of such a declarative act — whether independence is stated or produced by this utterance . . . This obscurity, this undecidability between, let's say, a performative structure and a constative structure, is *required* in order to produce the sought-after effect' (DI, 9). The very founding of a university, as of a research seminar calling itself Foreign Body, would thus be constituted in a fiction, by what Derrida terms 'a sort of fabulous retroactivity' (DI, 10) and by what he elsewhere describes as 'the impossibility for a principle of grounding to ground itself' (PR, 9).

I won't trouble you here with the full details, for example, of the extraordinary sort of post-card, that charter (*carta*) or post-charter which Her Majesty the Queen signed or countersigned on 14 December 1967 in response to what she calls 'an humble Petition [which] has been presented unto us by The University of Stirling Limited, being a company incorporated under the Companies Act, 1948, with the object inter alia of providing and carrying on in or near Our Royal Burgh of Stirling a University . . .'. Suffice to say that the impossibility and 'fabulous retroactivity' to which Derrida refers is evident in the very first so-called provision of this Charter, *viz*. '1. *There shall be and there is hereby constituted and founded* [my emphasis] in Our said County of Stirling and Royal Burgh of Stirling a University with the name and style of "The University of Stirling" (hereinafter called "the University").'[11] In its willingness to question and problematise its own institutionality and legitimacy, Foreign Body would be exemplary to the extent that such a willingness will, as Derrida puts it, 'have characterised *every* philosophical or scientific institution worthy of the name, that is to say, which has decided never to leave anything out of the question, not even its own institutional axiomatic' (Send, 17).

— Would that include, for example, the Cardiff critical theory seminar? Is that what you're talking about?

— You tell me.

— Did you say something?

— Like the university institution of which it both is and is not a part, Foreign Body is thus in its very inception haunted by fiction and by an experience of the impossible: calling into question *and* elaborating on its own strange but exemplary institutionality and legitimacy, it touches and tampers with 'the borders of language and of all the juridico-political contracts that it guarantees' (BL, 95).

— There is a foreign body in our midst.

— I have been calling it by this name, but it could be called something else, something altogether different.

— The invention of an institution.

— That's up to you.

— Who?

— You name it.

Notes

1 Samuel Beckett, *Waiting for Godot*, in *The Complete Dramatic Works* (London: Faber and Faber, 1986), 11.

2 I am grateful to Rachel Bowlby for alerting me to some of the curiosities of the motif of domestication attendant on deconstruction and its so-called reception in Anglophone universities.

3 See *JD i*, 254: 'no inside [is possible] without a relation to an outside which cannot be simply outside but must re-mark itself on the inside . . . [A]utonomy is de jure impossible'.

4 *Waiting for Godot*, 83.

5 Timothy Clark, *Derrida, Heidegger, Blanchot: Sources of Derrida's notion and practice of literature* (Cambridge: Cambridge University Press, 1992), 191.

6 For an account of the legalistic and theologico-political dimensions of footnotes, see Derrida's 'This Is Not an Oral Footnote', in *Anno-

tation and Its Texts, ed. Stephen A. Barney (Oxford: Oxford University Press, 1991), 192–205. Then burn this note (which I dedicate to Peter Buse and Peter Krapp).

7 Contributors to Foreign Body 'events' at the University of Stirling to date include Graham Allen, Valerie Allen, Ares Axiotis, Justin Bender, Mikkel Borch-Jacobsen, Julia Borossa, Scott Brewster, Lucille Cairns, Alan Campbell, John Drakakis, Diane Elam, Tom Furniss, Asko Kauppinen, Richard King, James Knowles, Naomi Liebler, Dan McAdam, Kirsteen McCue, Robert Maslen, Brian Matthews, Derek Mitchell, Hugh Osborne, David Punter, Ian Reader, Bill Readings, Caroline Rooney, Nicholas Royle, Grahame Smith, Mick Smith, Nigel Smith, Megan Stern, Rory Watson and Elizabeth Wright.

8 See E. S. Burt and Janie Vanpée, Editors' Preface, *Yale French Studies*, 77 (1990), 2.

9 Bill Readings, 'For a Heteronomous Cultural Politics: The University, Culture and the State', *Oxford Literary Review*, 15 (1993), 190.

10 In this context it may be suggested that the custodian of Foreign Body would be the figure neither of the professor nor of the (perhaps otherwise weirdly apposite) 'new blood' lecturer, but rather of the student, at least in the sense given to that term by Bill Readings when he writes: 'students know both that they are not yet part of culture and that culture is already over, precedes them. Neither nostalgia nor education can solve the students' malaise. They cannot simply mourn a lost culture (conservatism) nor can they forget the tradition and move on to build a bright new world (progressive modernism)' ('For a Heteronomous Cultural Politics', 189).

11 *University of Stirling Calendar 1993–94*, 53.

8

On not reading: Derrida and Beckett

One night as he sat trembling head in hands from head to foot a man appeared to him and said, I have been sent by — and here he named the dear name — to comfort you. Then drawing a worn volume from the pocket of his long black coat he sat and read till dawn. Then disappeared without a word.

Samuel Beckett[1]

Be alert to these invisible quotation marks, even within a word . . .

LO, 76

It may be said that, to date, there have been two broad characterisations of the work of Jacques Derrida. On the one hand it has been seen as primarily 'philosophical' and subsequently as seriously disruptive in relation to distinctions between the philosophical and the literary. The 'literary', that is to say, is here being thought from the side of or starting from the 'philosophical'. This characterisation is faithful to statements made by Derrida himself, for example when he speaks of the primary importance of being 'true to philosophy' (OCP, 218) or when he says that he always places himself 'in relation to philosophy' (IJD, 136).[2] On the other hand, there is the (mostly ill-informed) view of Derrida's work as basically 'literary' or 'non-philosophical' and subsequently as not seriously disruptive of anything much at all. In this chapter I wish to question both of these 'mainstream' perspectives, in particular by exploring the (perhaps differently disruptive) idea that Derrida's work might be considered from the perspective of being, in some curious way, not 'literary' *enough*. I acknowledge in advance the manifest folly of such an exploration. I feel it coming all the same. I will circle around three concerns:

not reading Derrida, not reading in Derrida's work, and Derrida not reading. In doing so I shall attempt to focus on the relationship between the writings of Derrida and Beckett and to consider (1) what might be involved in Derrida's professed inability to write about Beckett's work and (2), conversely, what light Beckett's work might cast on the question of reading and writing *after Derrida*.

Not reading Derrida

The recent and somewhat unusual Cambridge farce — about whether or not Jacques Derrida should be given an honorary degree by that university — highlighted once again, in English culture but no doubt also beyond it, the extraordinary importance of not reading. For it was clear that many of those opposing his nomination to this honorary degree — opposing him on the grounds that his work is 'nihilistic', 'unintelligible', 'meaningless' and so on — had not read Derrida's texts.[3] What is involved here? Even (or perhaps especially) if the writings of Derrida themselves remain unread, they have indelibly marked contemporary culture. A writer's work can be received without being read: texts have effects without being read.[4] Evoked here, then, is a sort of culture of hallucination, a culture of telepathy in which people's thoughts and values, their ideas and beliefs, are variously determined and dictated, transmitted and inscribed, by thinkers whose work has not been read.

Not reading in Derrida's work

Of course, there is not reading and there is not reading. Indeed it is in the reading and untangling of various figurations of 'not reading' that we might want to situate the importance of deconstruction. Deconstruction — which is never single or homogeneous, but which can here, at least provisionally, be identified with 'the work of Derrida' — is concerned with the lucid, patient attempt to trace what has not been read, what remains unread or unreadable within the elaboration of concepts and the workings of institutions. Frequently this concern has been construed by critics as the negative, irres-

ponsible or unethical character of deconstruction: deconstruction is concerned with nihilistically giving priority to the
unreadable.[5] In this respect, the unreadable corresponds to
the notion of the indeterminate. By way of trying to clarify a
fundamental misunderstanding of Derrida's work — characteristic, as we have seen, of criticism such as Geoffrey Hartman's, but also pervasive in the Cambridge affair — let us
merely propose that deconstructive thought is concerned not
with indeterminacy but rather with undecidability.

To classify a text, or a moment in a text, as indeterminate
is to put an end to the question of judging: it is, in a sense,
the opposite of undecidability. To talk about undecidability
is not to suggest that making decisions or judgements is
impossible but rather that any and every judgement is haunted by an *experience* of the undecidable, the effects of which
remain to be read. To refer to the meaning of a text, or a
moment in a text, as indeterminate is in fact to determine
a reading, to stop the process of reading. As Derrida summar-
ily observes in 'Living On', 'unreadability does not arrest reading' (LO, 116). To encounter the unreadable is not to bring
reading to an end, but rather to acknowledge the demand
that reading cannot stop, that reading begin again, that reading always and necessarily belongs to another time. Such an
acknowledgement is suggested by the aphorism from Pascal
about which Derrida speaks in *Mémoires*: 'When one reads
too swiftly or too slowly one understands nothing' (*M*, 88,
n.3).[6] This aphorism constitutes a kind of 'authoritative ellipsis' (*M*, 88, n.3) and evokes what is perhaps the most succinct
definition of deconstruction, that is to say 'the *experience of
the impossible*' (Aft, 200). 'When one reads too swiftly or too
slowly one understands nothing': to read this is at once
straightforward and impossible. The sentence must and
cannot be read at the right speed, according to a proper sense
of time. Aphorism in ruin, once again.

The unreadable is fixed only to the extent that it is apprehended as that which remains to be read, even if that reading
is theorised (as it is in Derrida's work) as belonging as much
to an immemorial past as to the future. An example of this
would be the piece of graffiti quoted by Derrida in 'Border
Lines': ' "do not read me" ' (BL, 145). This injunction must

and cannot be read. It is, as he points out, 'the sort of order that can be obeyed only by transgressing it beforehand' (BL, 145). This piece of graffiti concisely illustrates the double-bind of deconstruction, in other words the necessity and impossibility of deconstructive reading. It demands and dissolves the strange time, which is never proper, never *on* time, of reading. The reading of this injunction not to read can never catch up with itself, can never coincide with itself, not least because it can never have adequate authority to authorise its own reading (its 'authoritative ellipsis' is, again, also an ellipsis of authority) and because its very readability cannot be derived: what is readable is indissociable from what is iterable. The readable has no origin, it is immemorial, it precedes us and our reading.[7] By the same token the readable would be necessarily still to come.[8] It is still to come not as an act or event that might one day become present, but rather in the structural sense of a promise, a promise which is — in its affirmation and nonfulfilment — a double-bind.[9] In this sense, Derrida's work will never be readable. The reading of Derrida's texts is always still to come. If the readings advanced in the present study come after Derrida, they are by the same token still *after* Derrida in the sense of seeking after: reading 'after Derrida' can never arrive at itself.

Derrida not reading

Derrida has given seminars, in a 'stammering' fashion, on Beckett's work (see TSICL, 61). In the interview with Richard Kearney, published in 1984, he refers to Beckett in the context of the notion of literature, saying:

> when I speak of literature it is not with a capital L; it is rather an allusion to certain movements which have worked around the limits of our logical concepts, certain texts which make the limits of our language tremble, exposing them as divisible and questionable. This is what the works of Blanchot, Bataille or Beckett are particularly sensitive to. (DO, 112)

But Derrida has not (as yet) published work on Beckett and indeed has expressed an unwillingness, inability or avoidance in the face of such a prospect. We might wonder what is implied here. Is there some sense in which this professed inability might be seen as figuring a kind of fissure, or twilight zone, in Derrida's oeuvre?

Derrida's comments on his relation to the work of Beckett, in particular in the 1989 interview with Derek Attridge published in *Acts of Literature*, are somewhat enigmatic. Attridge asks Derrida why he has never written on Beckett. He responds:

> This is an author to whom I feel very close, or to whom I would like to feel myself very close; but also too close. Precisely because of this proximity, it is too hard for me, too easy and too hard. I have perhaps avoided him a bit because of this identification.... How could I write in French in the wake of or 'with' someone who does operations on this language which seem to me so strong and so necessary, but which must remain idiomatic? How could I write, sign, countersign performatively texts which 'respond' to Beckett? How could I avoid the platitude of a supposed academic metalanguage? (TSICL, 60)

No doubt the very form of an interview (so valuably and necessarily questioned around twenty years earlier, in *Positions*) tends to promote the kinds of 'platitude' to which Derrida refers, but the terms in which his relation to Beckett's work are being presented here are nevertheless provocative.

First, Derrida's remarks are strikingly author-centred. Beckett is 'an author' to whom he feels very close; Beckett is 'someone' who 'does operations' on the French language. However doomed to failure, my attempt to think about the writings of Beckett and Derrida in non-author-centred terms can perhaps be reinforced here by the fact that Beckett is no longer alive: his death, a few months after the Attridge–Derrida interview, casts an appropriate spectrality and passivity on the 'operations' to which Derrida refers. For it is, among other things, with precisely this spectral character of writing that the present study is preoccupied. Whether it is a question of Beckett or Derrida, Shakespeare or Toni Morrison, the focus here is on the ghostly, on the author as always already dead — that is to say, 'dead insofar as his text has a structure of survival even if he is living' (DTB, 183).

Second, and beyond the paradoxical claim of what is, in

Derrida's 'proximity' to 'Beckett', at once 'too easy' and 'too hard' (an ease or easiness which can in effect be neither proven nor refuted), there is this enigmatic appearance of the word 'but': 'How could I write in French in the wake of or "with" someone who does operations on this language which seem to me so strong and so necessary, but which must remain idiomatic?' How should we read (or perhaps, rather, *not* read) this 'but'? The strangeness of this 'but' (and the proviso of the 'idiomatic' which ensues) seems perhaps only to be increased when, a little later in the interview, and still on the question of 'Beckett', Derrida refers to the idiomatic dimension of his own writing. He is not concerned with reading, he says, even in the case of the works of Joyce, Celan or Blanchot: 'I will never claim to have "read" or proposed a general reading of these works. I wrote a text, which in the face of the event of another's text, as it comes to me at a particular, quite singular, moment, tries to "respond" or to "countersign", in an idiom which turns out to be mine' (62).

Derrida claims not to be able to 'respond' to Beckett's texts because they do not permit him what he calls 'writing transactions'. Consequently he concludes by saying: 'That wasn't possible for me with Beckett, whom I will thus have "avoided" as though I had always already read him and understood him too well' (61). What is going on in this, perhaps deceptively gentle and loving, appropriation?[10] What could it mean to have 'understood' Beckett 'too well'? What transformational forces of reading (or *not reading*) might be inscribed in this authoritative ellipsis, this peculiar abdication from reading what is nevertheless alleged to have been 'as though ... always already read'?

Not reading what not

Is it possible to read Beckett, even one or two words? Is it possible to read the word 'I', for example, or 'me', or not? Or what? What 'what'? And if not, what 'not'?

> Mr. Knott was a good master, in a way.
> Watt had no direct dealings with Mr. Knott, at this period.

> Not that Watt was ever to have any direct dealings with Mr.
> Knott, for he was not.[11]

Mastery and authority, including what Leo Bersani has called
'identity *as* authority',[12] is constitutively disabled, dislocated,
dispossessed in the fiction of Beckett. Engaged in a reading
of *The Unnamable*, for example, who are 'we'? The disturbance of identity is not only a matter of acknowledging, for
example, that our names carry death (in that they structurally
outlive their bearers) or that any 'operations' which we — as
readers or as writers — may carry out *in our names* are
likewise always already touched by the hand of death. For
the 'unnamable' referred to in the title of that text concerns
an unnamability affecting entitlement itself, the very entitlement of and to identity.[13] This logic pertains not only to the
'I' *in* the text but also to 'we', 'you', and 'they'. The notion of
identity is food, it could be said, not for thought but 'for
delirium'.[14] We/they are this text's constitutively multiple, irreducibly heterogeneous, anonymous, impossible readers:

> Do they believe I believe it is I who am speaking? That's theirs
> too. To make me believe I have an ego all my own, and can
> speak of it, as they of theirs. Another trap to snap me up among
> the living. It's how to fall into it they can't have explained to me
> sufficiently. (*U*, 348)

'I', 'they', 'we', and 'you' in turn are all ghosts within this
scene of reading.[15] There is no I to whom the speaking, writing
or reading of *The Unnamable* can be attributed. *The Unnamable*, more spectrally perhaps than any other work of twentieth-century literature *or* philosophy, calls for a reading that
would itself be unnamable, resistant to authority and identity
in general, contumacious (to evoke a 'nice image' (*U*, 383)) in
advance of every identification.

There would seem to be in Derrida's texts, on the other
hand, the recurrent deployment of a kind of implicit or
working assumption of the equation of identity-as-authority.
The deployment of the 'I' in Derrida's work, in this respect,
would appear to be radically different from that in Beckett's.
A brief consideration of some of the opening statements of
Derrida's texts may provide some indication of the regularity
with which they seem to start out with such a deployment,

even if they just as regularly proceed to a deconstruction or deconstitution of the identity of that 'I': 'I will speak, therefore, of a letter' (Diff, 3); 'Francis Ponge — from here I call him, for greeting and praise, for renown, I should say, or renaming' (S, 2); 'Genres are not to be mixed. I will not mix genres' (LG, 223); 'You might read these *envois* as the preface to a book that I have not written' (E, 3); 'What else am I going to be able to invent?' (PIO, 25); 'I have never known how to tell a story' (M, 3); 'I shall speak of ghost [*revenant*], of flame, and of ashes' (OS, 1); 'C'est ici un devoir, je dois *m'adresser* à vous en anglais. This is an obligation, I must *address* myself to you in English' (FL, 921). The narrator of *Murphy* famously observes: 'In the beginning was the pun'.[16] Even the phrase 'the fiction of Beckett' could be said to constitute a pun. The fictionality of authority — including or especially that of authorial identity, the writerly 'I' — would appear to set 'the fiction of Beckett' at odds with 'the work of Derrida'. Against the reading (or misreading) of Derrida as a 'punning', 'playful' (i.e. 'literary') writer, it might then seem possible to suggest that his texts are marked by a kind of literary 'insufficiency', a limiting of the 'literary' that renders itself readable through juxtaposition with the writings of Beckett.

To set out to suggest that Derrida's texts are not sufficiently 'literary' may seem like taking on the mantle of a somnambulist in a minefield. Quite apart from anything else, there is the danger of appearing to offer a 'strong reading', in the sense of that phrase glossed by David Wood: 'The paradox of *strong reading* is that it is strong precisely to the extent that it is not a reading, but the use of a sacrificial victim to exhibit one's own position.'[17] Wood's point makes sense so long as it is assumed that there is or can be such a thing as 'one's own position'. My concern here, however, has to do with the paradoxical, eerie but perhaps also laughable acknowledgement of a concern that can never be appropriated, never seriously be proposed as 'mine'. In this respect one must listen out for the pause that follows the somnambulist murmuring, 'Minefield? What minefield? There is no mine . . .' It is as the ghost of a somnambulist, then, that I reflect here on the concern with an 'unnamable', deconstructive reading of identity-as-authority, a reading that would identify (with) the space of literature as that which disables and dissolves the very possibility of 'one's own position'. This deconstructive reading is indeed, I would like to suggest, 'not a reading', but a kind of *not* reading at variance with what 'not' might be understood to mean in the context of Wood's formulation. It is with an elucidation of this rather different sense of 'not reading' that this essay will attempt to conclude.

A reading of the fiction of Beckett would appear to foreground the extent to which Derrida's writings deploy and rely on authority-effects (above all that of the identity-as-authority of an authorial 'I') which are dissolved and dispossessed, obliterated in the space of literature. Inevitably evoked here is the strange space of Maurice Blanchot's *The Space of Literature*, in which for instance we may read: 'The writer belongs to a language which no one speaks, which is addressed to no one, which has no centre, and which reveals nothing. He may believe that he affirms himself in this language, but what he affirms is altogether deprived of self'.[18] Such an account may be distinguished from the kind of 'space of literature' evoked by Derrida in 'This Strange Institution Called Literature', where literature is described as 'the institution which allows one to *say everything*' (36). Following Blanchot and Beckett, the space of literature might be characterised rather as that in which one loses the authoritative capacity to say 'one' at all. 'Where now? Who now? When now? Unquestioning. I, say I. Unbelieving' (*U*, 293): it may be said that these, the opening words of *The Unnamable*, 'must remain idiomatic', in other words resistant both to a 'strong reading' and even to the most gentle and loving appropriation, precisely to the extent that already, before starting, they will have dramatised the (fiction of the) unnamable, putting the 'I' into play as always already dispossessed, the authority of identity always already cast into question, dislocated, beyond belief.

Reading Beckett alongside or 'with' Derrida, then, tends to draw attention to the various ways in which Derrida's work seems to presuppose and impose the figure of a self-identical author or writer, valorising (even if it goes on to deconstitute) the inaugurating presence of the producer of 'writing transactions', the writerly 'I'. Such would appear to be the 'I', for example, which inaugurates the essay 'Force of Law: The "Mystical Foundation of Authority"' and which can later declare: 'I authorise myself — but by what right? — to multiply protocols and detours' (FL, 945). If, as has been suggested elsewhere, the subject of deconstruction is the deconstruction of the subject,[19] it may be recalled too that this deconstruction is a strategy without finality, a disseminatory strategy or series of strategies still being (and always still to be) elaborated and unfolded. It is a fundamental, if in some quarters still prevalent, misreading of Derrida's work to suppose that deconstruction is concerned with getting rid of the human subject. As he stresses, for example, in the interview with Richard Kearney, when he says: 'I have never said that the subject should be dispensed with. Only that it should be deconstructed... My work does not, therefore, destroy the subject; it simply tries to resituate it' (DO, 125).[20] In the twilight zone of the Beckettian reading that has been tentatively advanced here, however, it might be suggested that Derrida's work *does not go far enough* with its deconstruction of the subject, and that a deconstructive resituating of the subject calls to be further radicalised.

After Derrida: excitation

Complete madness. The madness of the day. A light unlike any other. I posthume as I breathe. Folly. Sheer kink. Nothing more or less than a folly to suggest that it could be appropriate to characterise Derrida's work in terms of a maintenance of identity as authority, of a legitimation of the violence of self-authorisation, of a persistence in valorising the writing 'I'. What is the word? Folly. In ruins. Beckett and Derrida, these two ghosts — each of them, like every ghost, double and more than double — are up to the same thing, in their different ways. If Beckett's work shows how — in Bersani's words — 'the strategies for continuing talk survive the absence of psychological subjects',[21] Derrida's work is likewise concerned with working through the deconstitution of psychological subjects, but *from the perspective of their presence*, from the experience of self-presence and, indeed, of *narcissism*. Derrida says as much, for example in that ghostly polyphonic text, 'Right of Inspection', which calls for 'a new understanding of narcissism, a new "patience", a new passion for narcissism'. The ghostly voice goes on: 'The right to narcissism must be rehabilitated, it needs the time and the means. More narcissism or else none at all [*Plus de narcissisme*]' (RI, 80).[22]

Beckett and Derrida: their laughter is almost indistinguishable. They repeat and repeat themselves, never the same. They give and efface themselves, these ghosts, with a humility, passion and patience that is at once inimitable ('like nobody else') and 'like nobody'.

It is time we disappeared. We, ghosts from another future.

We would like, finally, to disappear without a word, or at least with a word which, like the 'unnamable' or like 'deconstruction', may not be one. One way of trying to conceive of a practice of writing and reading after Beckett and after Derrida might be in terms of a theory of *excitation*. This term, in so far as it could be described as such (it would be no more a *term* than 'the unnamable' or 'deconstruction'), is pronounced so as to conceal as best it can the heterophonic pun it nevertheless harbours, like a foreign body. Excitation, that is to say, cannot be read without a logic of ex-citation, of that which dispossesses, ex-propriates or para-cites every citation. Excitation would have to do, among other things, with an absence of quotation marks. Be alert to these invisible quotation marks, even within a word: excitation. This would be the site, and sighting, of another apparent distinction between the ghostly I's, between Derrida and Beckett: Derrida's texts evince an almost constant pleasure in quotation and in the employment of quotation marks; Beckett's tend to avoid quotation marks altogether.[23] In Derrida's bizarre 'autobiothanatoheterographical' text entitled 'Circumfession', for example, we can read:

> and then I remember having gone to bed very late after a moment of anger or irony against a sentence of Proust's, praised in a book in this collection 'Les Contemporains', which says: 'A work in which there are theories is like an object on which one has left the price tag', and I find nothing more vulgar than this Franco-Britannic decorum, European in truth, I associate it with Joyce, Heidegger, Wittgenstein, and a few others, the salon litera-

ture of that republic of letters, the grimace of a good taste naive
enough to believe that one can efface the labor of theory, as if
there wasn't any in Pr., and mediocre theory at that. (*JD ii*, 62–3)

This passage not only presents a good example of Derrida's
liking for quotations (including, here, the citing of authorial
proper names) but also indicates the relentlessness with
which his own writing is concerned with 'theory' and with
making 'the labor of theory' explicit.

Of course to characterise Derrida's texts in terms of a
love for citation and quotation marks can only be done on
condition of acknowledging that these texts are at the same
time constantly, implacably engaged with showing how distinctions between quotation and non-quotation, use and mention, etc., are subject to a logic of contamination, of repetition
and difference, in other words subject to that which always
already destabilises citation, linking it to iterability.[24] A practice of writing after Derrida, that is to say a theory of excitation, might be figured in terms of a notion of passing into the
language. Recalling the question of reading and not reading
Derrida's work in relation to the idea of a culture of telepathy,
we might conclude by trying to take account of his suggestion,
made in *Mémoires*, that the 'ideal signature' is 'the one which
knows how to efface itself' (*M*, 26). The best signature would
be that which dissolves, no longer lets itself be read or lets
itself be read only as a kind of ghost. No longer the
(de)construction site of citation, but rather a space of excitation. Geoffrey Bennington's recent study of Derrida, 'Derridabase', which claims not to quote a single sentence of Derrida,
signals the way towards such a writing and such a theory. It
would no longer be necessary to cite Derrida: the most effective kind of writing after Derrida would be that in which
Derrida, the proper name, and everything ostensibly belonging to it, or presumed to enable a reader to read and identify
the singularity of a corpus (even that of a sentence) signed
'Derrida', had disappeared, passed into the language.[25] We
would return then, with an uncanny difference, to a notion of
'not reading Derrida'. This would be to envisage a kind
of fictional, theoretical writing, in other words, in which
'theory' has passed into the language.

Which is not to suppose that one could 'efface the labor of theory', as if there weren't any in Beckett (or Proust) — but rather to speculate on a theoretically vigilant, rigorous and inventive writing which would be radically excitational. Such a writing might seem, in some ways, closer to the work of Beckett than to that of Derrida, and yet it would be inconceivable without Derrida, without the telepathic hymen, the delirious excitation of both.

Notes

1 Samuel Beckett, 'Ohio Impromptu', in *The Complete Dramatic Works* (London: Faber and Faber, 1986), 447.

2 See too Derrida's illuminating comments on this topic in the interview with Derek Attridge entitled 'This Strange Institution Called Literature', where he compares literature and philosophy and meditates on the reasons for having been drawn personally and professionally to the latter. He reminisces on his unease about the 'innocence', 'irresponsibility' and 'impotence' of literature and his associating literature with 'the experience of a dissatisfaction or a lack, an impatience' (TSICL, 39). Philosophy on the other hand, he says, 'also seemed more political, let's say, more capable of posing politically the question of literature with the political seriousness and consequentiality it requires' (39). It should perhaps be added that, in what follows, I do not want to ignore or deny the extent to which Derrida's work is engaged, for example, with a mutual contamination of the philosophical and the literary, but rather I wish to continue an elaboration, initiated in *Telepathy and Literature: Essays on the Reading Mind* (Oxford and Cambridge, Mass.: Blackwell, 1991), of what happens if one tries (however perversely) to be 'true to literature', to place oneself primarily 'in relation to literature', and thus stage differently a certain priority of what might be called *not I*.

3 See, for example, Derrida's own remarks in this context, in 'An "Interview" with Jacques Derrida' (IJD), 131–9. Here he talks about the various 'distorting and malicious presentations' of his work and of those opponents to his degree nomination, 'whose every sentence proves clearly that they either haven't read or haven't understood one line of the texts they wish to denounce' (132).

4 In this context we might recall (though, for reasons by now perhaps sufficiently evident, without feeling obliged to endorse the rhetoric of mastery and discipleship marking it) a suggestion made by Paul de Man in 'Sign and Symbol in Hegel's *Aesthetics*', *Critical Inquiry*, 8

(summer 1982): 'Whether we know it, or like it, or not, most of us are Hegelians and quite orthodox ones at that . . . Few thinkers have so many disciples who have never read a word of their master's writings' (763).

5 For some particularly clear and stimulating refutations of such characterisations, see Derrida's 'Afterword: Toward an Ethic of Discussion' (ATED).

6 This aphorism is also of course the epigraph to Paul de Man's *Allegories of Reading: Figural Language in Rousseau, Nietzsche, Rilke, and Proust* (New Haven: Yale University Press, 1979).

7 See Derrida's remarks on 'How to Avoid Speaking', in *Languages of the Unsayable: The Play of Negativity in Literature and Literary Theory*, eds Sanford Budick and Wolfgang Iser (New York: Columbia University Press, 1989), 3–70. These remarks are perhaps also pertinent to any theory of reading, of not reading, or of how to avoid reading: 'Thus, at the moment when the question "How to avoid speaking?" arises, it is already too late. There was no longer any question of not speaking. Language has started without us, in us and before us. This is what theology calls God, and it is necessary, it will have been necessary, to speak. This "it is necessary" [*il faut*] is *both* the trace of undeniable necessity — which is another way of saying that one cannot avoid denying it, one can only deny it — *and* of a past injunction. Always already past, hence without a past present' (29).

8 See Samuel Weber, 'Reading and Writing *Chez* Derrida', in his *Institution and Interpretation* (Minneapolis: Minnesota University Press, 1987), 85–101. Weber notes that 'every text . . . is both structurally unreadable and yet destined to be read. It is structurally unreadable inasmuch as it can never be definitively delimited or situated (*casé*); it *is* only *as* the repetition of other readings, which in turn are the reinscription of other writings; and hence, the desire to repeat it for once and for all, to read it properly, is inevitably frustrated. And yet, at the same time, this desire is also unavoidable' (97–8).

9 This might be compared with Derrida's remarks in 'This Strange Institution Called Literature' on a concept of democracy as 'linked to the to-come [*à–venir*, cf. *avenir*, future], to the experience of a promise engaged, that is always an endless promise' (TSICL, 38). Cf. too Geoffrey Bennington's characterisation of politics as being '*now*, not projected into a utopian future, but in the event of the tension which is not to be *resolved*' (*JD i*, 257).

10 That reading and writing necessarily entail a double movement, a movement that is violent as well as loving, faithful and identificatory, is a consistent emphasis in Derrida's work. On the notion of practising a 'double writing' that is 'simultaneously faithful and violent',

for example, see *Positions* (*P*), 6. It is in the interviews in *Positions* also, we may recall, that Derrida emphasises what he calls 'The effective violence of disseminating writing' (85). The linking of violence and fidelity might further be compared with his comments on 'loving and violating' (TSICL, 61) language in the context of Beckett (and Artaud). Will the reading of Derrida offered here itself be construed as 'violating' as well as loving? Perhaps such an impression is unavoidable. But at the same time, and beyond this, I would also dare to hope that the present reading might be viewed as taking a little further, or approaching from another direction, Derrida's hypothesis in 'Afterword: Toward an Ethic of Discussion', that 'if . . . violence remains in fact (almost) ineradicable, its analysis and the most refined, ingenious account of its conditions will be the least violent gestures, perhaps even nonviolent, and in any case those which contribute most to transforming the legal-ethical-political rules: *in* the university and *outside* the university' (ATED, 112).

11 Samuel Beckett, *Watt* (London: John Calder, 1976), 64.

12 Leo Bersani, *The Culture of Redemption* (Cambridge, Mass.: Harvard University Press, 1990), 3.

13 This also applies to the notion of the identity of a national language: for a good account of some of the complexities of trying to think about Beckett's work in terms of 'operations' on a language, at once French and/or English but also irreducible to either, see Leslie Hill, *Beckett's Fiction: In Different Words* (Cambridge: Cambridge University Press, 1990), especially 40–58.

14 See Samuel Beckett, *The Unnamable*, in *Molloy, Malone Dies, The Unnamable* (London: Calder and Boyars, 1966), 337; hereafter cited in text as *U*.

15 See Leo Bersani and Ulysse Dutoit's recent reading of *Company* (in 'Beckett's Sociability', *Raritan*, 12:1 (summer 1992), 1–19), in which they suggest that ' "you" is also unnamable' (13) in this late text.

16 Samuel Beckett, *Murphy* (London: Picador, 1973), 41. Cited by Jonathan Culler in his Introduction to *On Puns: The Foundation of Letters* (Oxford: Blackwell, 1988), 16.

17 'Reading Derrida: An Introduction', in *Derrida: A Critical Reader*, ed. David Wood (Oxford and Cambridge, Mass.: Blackwell, 1992), 2.

18 Maurice Blanchot, *The Space of Literature*, trans. Ann Smock (Lincoln, Nebraska: Nebraska University Press, 1982), 26.

19 See, for example, Bill Readings, 'The Politics of Deconstruction', in *Reading de Man Reading*, eds. Lindsay Waters and Wlad Godzich (Minneapolis: Minnesota University Press, 1989), 241, n.24.

20 Cf. too 'Deconstruction in America: An Interview with Jacques

Derrida', in which he observes: 'the notion of "*writer*", and the notion of subject, *is* a logocentric product . . . The subject is a logocentric concept. That doesn't mean that we can get rid of it just like that. It's not a question of getting rid of it, moreover' (DA, 16).

21 *The Culture of Redemption*, 169.

22 For the paradox of this '*Plus de narcissisme*', cf. Derrida's remark, in 'Passions: "An Oblique Offering" ', that it is 'impossible to construct a non-contradictory or coherent concept of narcissism' (POO, 12).

23 Beckett's first novel *Murphy* (1938) would be the obvious exception to this rule. Interestingly, this pattern follows the work of Joyce: quotation marks are deployed in *Dubliners*, but not in *A Portrait*, *Ulysses* or *Finnegans Wake*.

24 See, in particular, 'Limited Inc' (LI) and 'Living On: Border Lines' (LO/BL).

25 Cf. Bennington's speculation at the end of 'Derridabase', regarding the absorption of Derrida 'into a textuality in which he may well have quite simply disappeared' (*JD i*, 316).

Index of names